The Architecture of
RICHTER & DAHL ROCHA

The Architecture of
RICHTER & DAHL ROCHA

with an essay by Jorge Francisco Liernur

BIRKHÄUSER – PUBLISHERS FOR ARCHITECTURE   BASEL · BERLIN · BOSTON

EDITED BY
Denise Bratton
Caroline Dionne

GRAPHIC DESIGN
Marco Turin

EDITORIAL DESIGN CONSULTANT
Janka Rahm

TRANSLATION
Ines Zalduendo

PROJECT COORDINATION
Caroline Dionne

PHOTOGRAPHY
Yves André
Mario Carrieri
Harmen Hoogland
Jean-Michel Landecy
Stéphane Spach
Olivier Wavre

ILLUSTRATIONS
Richter et Dahl Rocha, Bureau
d'Architectes SA, Lausanne,
Switzerland
Clestra Hauserman, Strasbourg,
France
Hevron SA, Courtételle,
Switzerland

Bibliographic information published by
Die Deutsche Bibliothek. Die Deutsche
Bibliothek lists this publication in the
Deutsche Nationalbibliografie; detailed
bibliographic data is available in the
internet at http://dnb.ddb.de

© 2007
Birkhäuser – Publishers for Architecture
P.O. Box 133
CH-4010 Basel, Switzerland
Part of Springer Science+Business Media

Printed on acid-free paper produced from
chlorine-free pulp. TCF ∞
Printed in Germany
ISBN-10: 3–7643–7599–X
ISBN-13: 978–3–7643–7599–7
9 8 7 6 5 4 3 2 1
www.birkhauser.ch

On Tact. Some Thoughts on the Architecture of Richter & Dahl Rocha   9
Jorge Francisco Liernur

On Tact. Some Thoughts on the Architecture of Richter & Dahl Rocha

Jorge Francisco Liernur (UTDT / CONICET)

Translated by Inés Zalduendo

*Si el fin del poema fuera el asombro, su tiempo no se mediría
por siglos, sino por días y por horas y tal vez por minutos.*
Jorge Luis Borges, "Averroë's Search" (1949) [1]

Premises

The dominant referents in contemporary architectural culture seem to be transforming the discipline into just another instrument of complicity in a world devoted
to the accelerated consumption of images. This is a world in which value seems
to reside only in perpetual novelty and difference, where a sound system might take
the shape of a ball, or a chair the form of a crab: The only constant is the demand
that such objects seduce consumers from the stylish windows of retail shops. Likewise, insofar as it ignores the legacy of historical modernisms, contemporary
architectural practice contributes to a frivolous form of play involving nonstandard
signifiers, like a skyscraper that resembles a gigantic pinecone or part of the
crust of a distant planet, a soccer stadium that looks like an enormous shoe or a
piece of exotic fruit, a school that recalls the site of an earthquake, or a museum
resembling a ship stranded at sea, glowing in the sunset.

Antonio Gramsci rightly asserted that "critical activity must be based on the
ability to make distinctions, to discover the difference underlying every superficial and apparent uniformity and likeness, and on the ability to discover the
essential unity underlying every apparent contrast and superficial differentiation."[2]
It is true that along with the most vocal figures in contemporary architecture,
Richter & Dahl Rocha comprehend the "essential unity" of architecture's nearly
complete structural integration with market forces. This is a pervasive condition,
one not unrelated to the belief (at least in the West) that "*la guerre est finie*," and
that 9/11 was just a horrific accident, even if a pivotal one. In this sense, the
architecture of Richter & Dahl Rocha is complicit with the contemporary architectural culture to which it belongs, largely characterized by a non-ideological attitude
quite far removed from the milieu of a century ago when one had to choose
between Architecture and Revolution. But, beyond that "essential unity" with the

1 "Averroë's Search," trans. Andrew Hurley, *Jorge Luis Borges Collected Fictions* (New York: Viking Penguin, 1998),
p. 240: "if the purpose of the poem were to astound, its life would not be measured in centuries but in days, or hours,
or perhaps even minutes"; "La busca de Averroes," was originally published in Jorge Luis Borges, *Obras completas*
(Buenos Aires: Emecé Editores, 1949), p. 586.
2 Antonio Gramsci, "Some Criteria of 'Literary' Judgment," *Selections from Cultural Writings: Problems of Criticism*,
ed. David Forgacs and Geoffrey Nowell-Smith, trans. William Boelhower (Cambridge, Mass.: Harvard University Press,
1985), p. 232; originally published in *Letteratura e vita nazionale* (Turin: Einaudi, 1975), p. 37.

architects of their time, it soon becomes apparent that the work of Jacques Richter and Ignacio Dahl Rocha shares almost no common ground with the great infrastructural gestures of architects who celebrate globalization in a transparent (and even banal) manner; nor do they share the current passion for an architecture based on the equivocal forms emerging from computer screens to ignite the imagination of young students (as well as not-so-young architects), or the already rather outmoded taste for seismic disasters.

The singularity of the architecture of Richter & Dahl Rocha resides precisely in the fact that it does not call attention to its "originality." However, before it can be dismissed as just another *déjà vu*, it reveals a subtle resonance that may not be perceived at first glance. In contrast to the potent images proffered in mainstream architecture magazines, which capture the reader's interest in an aggressive way, the resonance that we perceive in the work of Richter & Dahl Rocha demands from the beholder a sustained effort to comprehend it. And what is interesting about the work is that it achieves this subtle resonance by situating itself in a liminal space determined by the architects' refusal to abandon the archaic realm of Architecture itself, and their resistance to the exaggerated rhetoric and histrionics of the mass media. They achieve this without losing sight of the field of practice defined by programs, modes of production, and public as well as private patronage. It is in the work's ability to maintain this tenuous balance, almost to the point of its own disappearance, that we discover its appeal.

It has been suggested that, in its rejection of garishness, the architecture of Richter & Dahl Rocha identifies with what has come to be called the "new simplic-ity" in Swiss architecture.[3] But it seems to me more fruitful to pursue Gramsci's other injunction, "to discover the difference underlying every superficial and appar-ent uniformity and likeness," precisely because the architecture of Richter & Dahl Rocha is far from "simple." This is not a function of rhetoric or intentionality, the aesthetic or typological character of the work, or its constructional qualities. If it were not for their commitment to the specificity of the discipline of architecture, the "silence" of Richter & Dahl Rocha's work could perhaps be construed as an absence of meaning – a gesture that is typically the purview of artists who operate in fields where their work is evaluated in purely formal terms, where it is a matter, as Frank Stella famously commented, of "what you see" and only "what you see." The overwhelming majority of architects are never called upon to propose "unique" buildings to ornament global capital cities, to put unknown towns "on the map," or to promote the aesthetic avant-gardism of progressive business moguls. Like Richter & Dahl Rocha, most architects manage to operate within a certain range of opportunities and challenges, but few manage to capitalize on the resources at hand in order to channel them into works of Architecture.

But, how does one reveal a delicate nuance without canceling it? How does one arrest for a moment the fleeting sensation that has been calculated precisely to elude overt attention? In his essay on "Goethe's Elective Affinities," Walter Benjamin offered an appealing suggestion, which, taking a cue from Carlo Ginzburg, we could call a "knight's move": "Let us suppose that one makes the acquaintance

---

3 See Stanislaus von Moos, *Minimal Tradition: Max Bill und die "einfache" Architektur, 1942–1996 / Max Bill et l'architecture "simple," 1942–1996* (Baden: Bundesamt für Kultur im Verlag Lars Müller, 1996).

of a person who is handsome and attractive but impenetrable, because he carries a secret with him. It would be reprehensible to want to pry. Still, it would surely be permissible to inquire whether he has any siblings and whether their nature could not perhaps explain somewhat the enigmatic character of the stranger. In just this way the critique seeks to discover siblings of the work of art."[4] To put this suggestion into practice entails approaching the work at several of its constituent levels, and to do so knowing that even if we are not able to disclose the heart of the secret (because of course it is in its absolute inviolability that the fascination resides), we will at least be able to establish some points of reference capable of sparking the reader's own intuitions. In this sense, it should be made clear that my essay does not belong to the architectural work being presented in this monographic volume.

As an autonomous act, critical writing constitutes an attempt to cast creative work in its cultural context, where it crosses paths with other institutions and agents including the reader, who brings to it his or her own experiences and opinions. For our purposes, criticism thus constitutes another episode in the process of generating the layers of meaning that accrue to a work of architecture. As Michael Speaks has framed the point: "If we understand writing as production and not as an essence at the center of which is the word, then writing becomes architectural not according to what it is but to what it does: writing becomes architectural by producing architecture... In a real sense, then, institution architecture is a production cycle, an invisible architectural built form that grows with each sentence, review, criticism, and book."[5]

With this reference I merely want to imply the existence of a semantic gap that has come to exert the power of a "force field" between the realm of building and that of the written word. It is in this charged field that the body of work represented here plays its role.

✳

Switzerland | Argentina
One of the distinguishing aspects of Richter & Dahl Rocha's work is the nature of the programs to which it responds. Generally speaking, it does not aspire to the rhetorical expression of public or private entities. Instead, it focuses on residential complexes and commercial, industrial, and educational facilities. Of nearly 40 projects developed by Richter & Dahl Rocha since its foundation in the early 1990s, 10 have been the result of competitions, while the rest were commissioned by corporations, real estate developers, government entities, banking institutions, insurance companies, schools, and a few private individuals. In a number of cases, works were commissioned by the same client at different moments in time. From this summary description and a cursory glance at the work, it is safe to make three initial observations. First, private commissions represent the majority of Richter & Dahl Rocha's projects, which, if

---

4 Walter Benjamin, "Goethe's Elective Affinities" (1919–1922), trans. Stanley Corngold, *Walter Benjamin: Selected Writings, Volume 1, 1913–1926*, ed. Marcus Bullock and Michael W. Jennings (Cambridge, Mass. & London: The Belknap Press of Harvard University Press, 1999), p. 333; originally published as "Goethes Wahlverwandtschaften," *Neue Deutsche Beiträge* 2/1 (1925): 38, and 2/2 (1925): 134.
5 Michael Speaks, "Writing in Architecture," *ANY* 0 (May-June 1993): 6.

we apply the standard cliché of criticism, do not seem compatible with Architecture.[6] Second, although at first sight most of the work falls into the general category of "commercial" production, the sheer number of their projects generated by architectural competitions defies this label. And third, with the exception of a few projects, Richter & Dahl Rocha's commissions have not been driven by the client's explicit demand for architectural "discourse" or quality. This is to say that the quality which I feel is intrinsic to their built work was produced mostly *in spite of* market forces, which in many instances respond to a quite another logic.

Let us briefly examine the context into which the work inserts itself, and on which it depends, and the ways in which Richter and Dahl Rocha's own histories are entwined with it. The firm's growth coincided with the slow cycle of recovery from Switzerland's "identity crisis," which reached its height during Expo 1992 in Seville, when the Swiss identified with the slogan *"La Suisse n'existe pas."* Internationally, this crisis reached a crescendo in the mid-1990s, with Switzerland rejecting the bid to join the European Union and simultaneously being censured for its hitherto unrecognized role in the Holocaust.[7] On the occasion of the opening of Expo 2002, President Kaspar Villiger acknowledged as much: "The 1990s were in fact difficult: economic stagnation, unemployment at record levels, criticism of Switzerland for its conduct during the Second World War, and difficult negotiations with the European Union... One is moved to speak of nothing if not a crisis of identity."[8] The publication of this book, which presents a sophisticated, coherent, and mature body of work attesting to an uncompromising project spanning this very same period, comes at a moment when the trends Villiger described seem to have been reversed – despite the fact that for some, the Swiss identity crisis has not yet been resolved, especially with respect to the notion of a common social project.[9]

Such matters are consequential for our purposes, inasmuch as Switzerland's recovery has occurred in parallel with changes affecting the construction industry, and thus the character and number of programs and requirements that determine architectural production. Globalization and the advance of a market economy into spheres that were formerly the province of the government have also had an impact which is to some extent reflected in bilateral agreements between Switzerland and the European Union. To begin with, this has spurred private commissions. Between 1975 and 2001, when public spending for new construction declined slightly, privately commissioned construction increased by more than 10,000 million

6   There is some truth to this cliché. It is not by chance that in the United States, the term is generally reserved for describing the architecture of university campuses or highly profitable cultural enterprises, while in Spain during recent years, extremely high-quality production generated under the auspices of government commissions (national, regional, and local) has become the norm.

7   Among other sources, see Jean Ziegler, *La Suisse lave plus blanc* (Paris: Éditions Du Seuil, 1990); Jürg Altwegg, *Une Suisse en crise* (Lausanne: Presses Polytechniques et Universitaires Romandes, 2004); and Claude Mossé, *La Suisse, c'est foutu. Une espèce à part* (Monaco: Éditions du Rocher, 2003). It is also important to remember that several pivotal events effectively disrupted the long-standing image of Switzerland as an impartial and infallible "world apart." I refer of course to the Zug massacre, the bankruptcy of Swissair, and the almost simultaneous accident and fire in the Gotthard tunnel.

8   Founded in 1883, the Swiss Expo was held at intervals of 13, 24, 25, and 25 years until 2002, when it had been 38 years since the previous one was celebrated.

9   According to advertising executive Dominique von Matt, Switzerland is appreciated anew after the depression phase of the 1990s. It is perceived more positively from a foreign point of view than from within. In September 2001 – shortly before the attacks – a study conducted by the Swiss Federal Institute of Technology (ETH) in Zurich revealed that the Swiss population felt better, and safer, than ever.

Swiss Francs.[10] According to some analysts, transformations wrought by globalization have affected the entire country, tending to organize it not as an urban, but rather a metropolitan network around the five big agglomerations of Zurich, Basel, the Ticino, Berne, and Geneva, which are of course closely related to Milan, Lyon, Munich, and Stuttgart.[11] These agglomerations seem to be transforming the very nature of settlements in Switzerland in a process that has come to be known as "rurbanization," whereby rural land uses are articulated with urban, industrial, and touristic uses throughout the country. Likewise, a more intensive use of existing built fabric is being expressed in the revitalization of declining urban centers, as well as an increase in renovations, additions, and adaptive re-use, albeit at the expense of new construction. In fact, throughout the 1980s and 1990s, the market for new construction of residences declined 50%. In addition, significant changes in the type of dwellings being produced during this period have resulted in two- and three-room apartments being outpaced by single-family houses and larger apartments of five to six rooms, along with a marked shift from mass-produced housing in suburban areas to smaller developments in already urbanized areas.[12]

In addition to such changes in demand, the introduction of new material and information technologies has brought about transformations in the organizational structure and profile of many architecture offices. Not least of these is the increasing number of emerging architects who leave their jobs with mid-sized to large architectural firms in order to open independent studios.[13] The combined effect of the increase in private commissions and recent transformations in production and construction modes in many cases encourages specialization. Under such conditions, it is understandable that critics might conclude that "the relative decline of the traditional craft-based office raises questions concerning the durability of the ethical principles that have for a long time guided the practice of independent architects," and point to "another crucial problem: doesn't the quality of services provided by architects to their community become illusory in light of the inevitable fragmentation of responsibility that results from the disappearance of the architect as sole manager of all building operations?"[14]

By Swiss standards, Richter & Dahl Rocha is considered to be a "large" firm,[15] but it has opted neither to specialize, nor to establish itself as a corporation. In response to the rise in private commissions, Richter & Dahl Rocha has managed to maintain a commitment to craftsmanship and centralized responsibility characteristic of traditional architectural production. The organzational structure of the office, with an executive management group overseeing various project "teams" headed by Richter & Dahl Rocha associates, has proven to be a viable formula for sustaining

---

10 Public spending for construction declined from 6,528 to 6,129 million Swiss Francs, while private construction increased from 18,100 to 28,414 million.

11 See Michel Bassand, *La metropolization de la Suisse* (Lausanne: Presses Polytechniques et Universitaires Romandes, 2004).

12 See André Ducret, Claude Grin, Paul Marti, Ola Söderström, *Architecte en Suisse. Enquête sur une profession en chantier* (Lausanne: Presses Polytechniques et Universitaires, 2003).

13 According to Ducret, et alia, investments in construction decreased between 1990 and 2001 from 41,183 to 34,543 million Swiss Francs, in an inverse relation to an increase in the number of architecture offices from 6,500 in 1985 to 10,000 in 2001; see *Architecte en Suisse*, p. 46.

14 Ducret, et alia, *Architecte en Suisse*, p. 60.

15 In Switzerland large practices employ between 50 and 499 full-time employees. Ducret, et alia, *Architecte en Suisse*, p. 53 (our translation).

the delicate balance between creativity and invention on the one hand, and the conscious and efficient management of time and resources on the other.

Descriptions of the firm have drawn attention to its multinational character as one of its great strengths. There are currently 50 individuals from 12 different countries, of which 15 hold diplomas in architecture. Of those, five are technical architects, eight are project managers, seven are draftspeople, and seven are administrative staff, with a varying number of assistants. The variety of backgrounds they bring to the office results in a stimulating mix of viewpoints, as the editors of *Architecture Suisse* have aptly observed: "Despite the fact that it takes root, culturally and professionally, in the local milieu, the work of Richter & Dahl Rocha makes way for the "other," for this difference that is the result of a multicultural dialogue, to subtly show through. This condition gives their architecture a particular identity that makes it difficult to label. Although conscious, it does not appear to be voluntary or explicit. Rather, it can be seen as the inevitable consequence of genuine teamwork that is concerned with concrete local problems while involving collaborators who have very different approaches to reality."[16]

However it is difficult to draw from this "cosmopolitan" condition of the office something that distinguishes the work of Richter & Dahl Rocha from other firms of its size. It is relatively common in the age of globalization for an architecture office to be composed of collaborators of many nationalities. Likewise, it is not uncommon to find the partners of prominent firms coming from different countries than those in which each shaped and developed his or her identity as an architect. Emigration is a fact of contemporary life, with people moving in all directions. What is not so common is a lasting partnership between two protagonists stemming from such fundamentally different contexts. Jacques Richter and Ignacio Dahl Rocha first crossed paths at Yale University. What could a young man who had lived through the dark turbulence that characterized Argentina during the 1970s have in common with one who was brought up in the secure and affluent environment of the Alpine Confederation of Switzerland?

Take Richter's case. As is well known, architecture in Switzerland is strongly conditioned by stringent building codes, the democratic participation of its citizens in urban matters, and cutting-edge technology in the building industries. Within this context, and particularly with respect to work for large corporations, the margin for creativity is reduced in the extreme. In this sense, Stanislaus von Moos' characterization of Max Bill also resonates in the work of Richter & Dahl Rocha: "In contrast to other "quality architecture" of its time, Bill was not averse to letting his buildings merge with their quotidian context: a project for a radio station or a house of his, inserted among the railway tracks, industrial complexes, and middle-class residential complexes of Switzerland – not unlike the places documented in the photos and videos of Peter Fischli and David Weiss celebrating the banality of contemporary life – might almost go unnoticed."[17]

But these same conditions characterize most architecture produced in Switzerland, and therefore do not set Richter & Dahl Rocha apart. Richter's education was grounded in the so-called Swiss "modern tradition," which was

16   See "Un bureau face à la pluriculturalité," *Architecture Suisse* 152 (January 2004): 1.
17   Stanislaus Von Moos, "Max Bill: A la búsqueda de la 'cabaña primitiva'," *2G* (2004): 29f.

formulated in the 1930s and officially advanced with the publication of Alfred Roth's *La Nouvelle Architecture, Présenté en 20 examples* (1946). This "tradition" constitutes a lesson in "responsible" modernism, a credible, non-confrontational response to the sustainability of new architectures within the stable social and economic background of Switzerland. With its attention to materials, quality of construction, rational and functional organization, and the elegant manipulation of form, the Swiss modern tradition has manifestly rejected the simplistic notion of regionalism. Above all, it has rejected both the revolutionary rhetoric and the excessive formalism of other European modernisms. But within the history of modern architecture in Switzerland, a number of the trajectories that cut across this tendency to formal restraint are, on the other hand, among the most extreme expressions of the avant-garde – from the work of Le Corbusier himself to the projects, works, and proposals of the ABC group. In addition, Jacques Richter's path included, of course, the "American" experience at Yale, and looking back, one sees that certain pivotal developments in his career stem precisely from that period.

To begin with, the architectural tradition in the "Romande" or French-speaking region of Switzerland is distinct from that of the other cantons. One could say that, while the experience of German- or Italian-speaking Swiss architects is inherently tied to the most extreme, turbulent, and even "revolutionary" histories of German and Italian modernisms respectively, those of the French-speaking region belong to a different history. This is a history that resisted modern architecture's sudden break with the Academy in France, and came to be associated not only with the architecture of Alberto Sartoris, Henri-Robert Von der Muhll, and even the Honneger brothers, Georges and Auric. In this context, Adolphe Guyonet or Le Corbusier in Geneva represented exceptions. Marc Piccard's Bellerive-Plage beach and pool complex in Lausanne stands as evidence that it was well into the 1930s before "modern architecture" in its most committed versions began to merge with the local culture of the Romande region. Geneva architectural historian Jacques Gubler has gone so as far as to assert that "the French part of Switzerland seems much less willing to accept new architecture due to the ultra-reactionary 'poetic penchant' of its intelligentsia – the Federation of Swiss Architects (FAS) included."

In broad terms, the conservatism of modern Switzerland has been repeatedly explained as a result of the dominant role of banking institutions in the country's economy. According to Jürg Altwegg, the Swiss are "always very conservative in politics, because they invest with an eye to the long term; their major business ventures can only prosper in the context of a stable social system."[18] Making reference to the manner in which that conservatism is expressed as an "aesthetic of restraint," Altwegg quotes the Swiss banker Edouard Pictet, for whom Calvinism in Geneva "is a matter of consciousness. One is more or less comfortable financially, more or less wealthy, but this does not justify extravagant gestures. On the contrary, one remains modest. Even if it is not a matter of necessity, one remains thrifty. One does not attend a theatre play wearing diamonds because one can afford it. This would be inappropriate. We refuse the looks and everything that trivially evokes the '*nouveau riche*'…. We despise garish, superficial signs of wealth."[19]

18 Altwegg, *Une Suisse en crise*, p. 12 (our translation).
19 Ibid., p. 18 (our translation).

However, by focusing on qualities such as "restraint" and "conservatism," one risks losing sight of the fact that, on the contrary, strong currents of change have also swept across the Romande region. In fact, this was where Switzerland's entry into the European Union was approved in a referendum, while the rest of Switzerland decided to reject the option. Oppositional positions taken by certain of the region's intellectuals are also indicators of open-mindedness. Denis de Rougemont, founder of the European Center for Culture in Geneva, "violently criticized Switzerland," but on the other hand noted that "the country's history and political structure, as well as its multilingual character, represented, in many respects, a parallel to the unified Europe he envisioned." Alfred Berchtold characterized Romande Switzerland as "a land of bridges and valleys, which, if it does not open itself to the outside, does not exist."[20]

The initial eclecticism or neutrality of the Romande Swiss modernists during the decades following the Second World War enabled the region to embrace other international expressions more openly than the rest of Switzerland. One example of this was of course the remarkable work of Jean Tschumi, particularly, as Isabelle Charollais and Bruno Marchand have proposed, insofar as it struck "a delicate balance between functionality and representation, between modernism and Beaux-Arts tradition."[21] This was also the case with the work of Max Richter and Marcel Gut, which naturally had impact on Jacques Richter's education and development as an architect. The office of Richter & Gut, on whose foundations Richter & Dahl Rocha was initially organized, was one of the most distinguished in Romande Switzerland during the 1960s and 1970s, both in terms of its sheer volume of production and the professional quality of the work. Theirs was a consistent architecture, an architecture initially marked by a Corbusian influence (as evidenced in their boarding school at Valmont completed in 1964), which subsequently incorporated an American Brutalism inspired by Paul Rudolf and Richard Neutra, as evinced in their La Placette Commercial Center in Vevey of 1973.

Jacques Richter pursued his architectural degree at the Swiss Federal Institute of Technology (ETH), Zurich, in the 1970s, at a moment when Aldo Rossi was a strong presence and the "Ticino school" was in the ascendant in Switzerland. Richter identified with the Tendenza movement, and eventually headed to the United States in search of the Kahnian roots of "rationalism" at Yale. There, as we know, he met his future partner. Dahl Rocha's decision in favor of equilibrium and restraint had a very different pitch.

Modern architecture in Argentina is less well understood internationally than its Swiss incarnations, but as the product of a country and culture that flourished during the early decades of the 20th century, it attained an unusual degree of richness. It was the force of modernization in Argentina that attracted Le Corbusier when he made his first trip to the Americas in 1929.[22] The cosmopolitan character of the great urban centers of the Río de la Plata region bear witness to a sophisticated

20 Altwegg, *Une Suisse en crise*, p. 43; and Alfred Berchtold, *La Suisse romande au cap du XXe siècle. Portrait litteraire et moral* (Lausanne: Payot, 1980).
21 Isabelle Charollais and Bruno Marchand, "Entre représentativité et fonctionnalité," *Faces* 39 (Fall 1996): 50.
22 Le Corbusier visited Buenos Aires in 1929, when he was invited by a group of institutions at the instigation of

interweaving of disparate cultures, whose heterogeneity cannot be explained within simplistic Euro-North-American schemas that use to find in Latin America an "other" clearly differentiated by "magic realism." The urban culture of the Río de la Plata region established itself as an outcome of immigration, modernization, and literacy. A society composed of multiple nationalities grew up, educated under the direction of a local elite who developed a neutral modernism as a means of homogenizing the country's plurality, and was preoccupied with establishing "one" identity, and with it, "one" nation.

The modernist architectural ethos inherited by Dahl Rocha above all derives from a system of quality and representation comprising the landscape of Argentine cities. It is important to stress that it indeed comprised a *system*, and not a group of exceptions like those occurring at other latitudes on the continent.[23] Alberto Prebisch, Vladimiro Acosta, Sánchez, Lagos y De la Torre, but above all Antonio Vilar best expressed the modern tradition in Argentina, which reached its height in the 1940s with the work of the Spanish exile Antonio Bonet, Juan Kurchan, and Jorge Ferrari Hardoy – whose so-called "butterfly" chair (named BKF after the three of them) epitomized modernist furniture. From the rigorous creative path of Amancio Williams to the contemporary work of Mario Roberto Alvarez, this tradition of innovation flourished alongside the pursuit of an architecture of quality matched by extreme restraint and accompanied by resistance to the label of "regional modernism." And it has continued to evolve within the context of a contemporary Argentine culture dominated by a minimalist paradigm that sublimates practical and metaphysical realities imposed by the enormous plain of the Pampa and the infinite horizon of the mythical *rio-mar*, the great river-sea that flows downstream across the plain where it becomes so shallow that one can walk across it for kilometers.

Dahl Rocha absorbed this tradition while working with Ernesto Katzenstein, a disciple of Bonet and nephew of Vilar. A magnificent figure within Argentine architecture circles at the end of the 20th century, Katzenstein was steeped in an almost mystical (but decidedly secular) belief in the need for restraint. For him, it was no longer as a means of homogenizing diversity, but rather as a critique of the noisy and banal rhetoric typical of his own society and time.[24] To this search for aesthetic restraint during those dark years, in what can only be described as a "gagged" society, was added an acute awareness of the inevitable distortion of any voice that dared to speak out. Under the military dictatorship of General Videla,

Victoria Ocampo, a member of the Argentine social and cultural elite. During that trip, he also visited Uruguay and Brazil. The most significant consequences were his proposals for Buenos Aires, Montevideo, São Paolo, and Rio de Janeiro. In 1938, Le Corbusier hosted two young Argentine architects who were visiting Paris, Jorge Ferrari Hardoy and Juan Kurchan. With his collaboration, the proposals for Buenos Aires were transformed into a Plan, and as a result a CIAM group called "Austral" was founded in Buenos Aires with the participation of former disciple of Le Corbusier and Joseph Lluis Sert, Antonio Bonet. In 1948, the municipality of Buenos Aires created a special office to develop the Plan, and in the same year, Le Corbusier began the project for Dr. Curutchet's house in La Plata, 70 kilometers from the city. This and the Carpenter Center in Boston are Le Corbusier's only two buildings in the Americas.

23   I am referring to familiar examples such as the so-called "Brazilian miracle" of the 1940s and 1950s, embodied in the figures of Oscar Niemeyer and Lúcio Costa, or the more individualistic example of Carlos Raúl Villanueva in Venezuela; cfr. Jorge F. Liernur, "'The South American Way'. El 'milagro' brasileño, los Estados Unidos y la Segunda Guerra Mundial (1939-1943)," *Block* 4 (1999): 23–41.

24   See Jorge F. Liernur, "La importancia de ser Ernesto," *Ernesto Katzenstein Arquitecto* (Buenos Aires: Fondo Nacional de las Artes, 1998).

Dahl Rocha was a student of the unofficial school where Katzenstein and his colleagues were trying to construct space of architectural culture and thought.[25]

It was in this context that I met him. He had not yet finished his formal studies, but his exceptional creative talent and the openness of his theoretical curiosity were already evident. The leap to Kahn's Yale was a necessary step in his search for a tolerant cultural environment where that curiosity could be nourished by exposure to contemporary developments and tested in a stable economic context. Here, as we know, began the "Swiss" stage of Ignacio Dahl Rocha's career.

This intellectual pilgrimage from the Pampa to the Alps may seem anomalous, but it is not so unusual. Crossing the ocean in the opposite direction during the summer of 1914, the family of Jorge Luis Borges arrived in Geneva, where they lived for five years at the Rue Ferdinand Hödler while Borges and his siblings attended high school at the Collège Calvin. Borges felt so deeply connected to the city that he returned to it, almost *incognito*, at the end of 1985, died there, and was buried there in the Pleinpalais Cemetery on June 14 of the following year. Needless to say, before Borges' time, many Swiss Romande *emigrés* had already discovered a quality of life in Argentina that their own country could not offer. And it should not be forgotten that Richter and Dahl Rocha's story was itself prefigured during the 1940s, when Max Bill and the Argentinean Tomás Maldonado engaged in a productive exchange of ideas. However, in contrast to the case of Richter and Dahl Rocha, Bill and Maldonado committed themselves to the quest for one "good" solution for the totality of visual culture.

What characterizes Richter & Dahl Rocha is thus not only the multinational composition of the office, but also the permanent state of tension in which their partnership exists, cultivated by Richter's commitment to open-mindedness, and inspired by the "otherness" that Dahl Rocha brought to Switzerland from a land rife with contradiction, from the banks of that vast and remote river in which one could see snakes floating downstream from the jungle, crossing icebergs that the wind carries from the frozen southern seas.

✳

"Architectum ego hunc fore constituam, qui certa admirabilique ratione et via tum mente animoque diffinire tum et opera absolvere didicerit, quaecunque ex ponderum motu corporumque compactione et coagmentatione dignissimis hominum usibus bellissime commodentur."
Leon Battista Alberti, *On the Art of Building in Ten Books* (c. 1452)[26]

Spectacle versus Architecture
Death is the inevitable destiny of all that is human, and Architecture is no exception. It may seem to be a banal statement, but philosophers from Hegel onward have offered ever more sophisticated arguments to confirm its truth. More cogently than any other critic of the last half of the 20th century, Manfredo Tafuri expressed this tragic destiny, bringing to it his acute intelligence and sophisticated theoretical

25 Justo Solsona, Antonio Diaz, and Rafael Viñoly.
26 *On the Art of Building in Ten Books* (1450), trans. Joseph Rykwert, Neil Leach, and Robert Tavernor (Cambridge, Mass.: The Mit Press, 1988), prologue, in which Alberti describes the architect as he "who by sure and wonderful reason and method, knows both how to devise through his own mind and energy, and to realize by construction,

tools. One of the most recent incarnations of his funerary prediction relates to the shapeless digital products known as "blobs," a cultural phenomenon which, as Kazys Varnelis has suggested, may indeed be advancing with great speed toward its own exhaustion: "When the blob becomes banal, the last formal monument will come to an end, and architecture itself will be able to disappear. In exploring the remaining geometries that architecture previously could not conceive or build, the blob marks the end of formal movements in architecture. With these having exhausted themselves, we reach the end of architectural form."[27]

That the product of these articulations between new digital media, architects, and the marketplace would lead toward a cataclysmic end (or at least profound consequences for architecture) has been predicted by critics from the traditional sector. Under the direction of Kurt Forster, the 9th Architecture Biennale in Venice was driven by the quest to understand the new state of things presented under the title *Metamorphosi*: "We have developed a line of arguments about the recent transformations in the nature of architecture itself. Our hypothesis is based on the special nature of those transformations. In the last quarter-century or so, architecture has not only changed, as it always does, in diverse and often unpredictable ways, it also begun to transform itself. These changes are so profound as to suggest a transformation of the very species of architecture whose different properties can only be discovered in retrospect. One might say that when some fish began to emerge from the sea and develop limbs, or when reptiles grew skin and feathers on their legs, they turned into birds."[28] Forster's observation could be correct, that is, it may be true that ours is an era in which the reptile is starting to grow feathers. There is some consensus that a cluster of new activities and modes of organization involving architects is emerging. Validating Robert Venturi's motto, it has even been asserted that "the architect is going to be the fashion designer of the future. Learning from Calvin Klein, the architect will be concerned with dressing the future, speculating, anticipating coming events, and holding up a mirror to the world."[29] In the context of this transformation, Architecture/the reptile would be metamorphosing into a spectacle/the bird. Stronger in each instance, whether in the form of "fashion design" or under the pressure of image consumption on the part of architecture schools or advertising at a global scale, the task of architects is rapidly evolving in the direction of branding.

However, even if Forster's observation seems accurate, we may not agree with his conclusions. Darwin simply held that species tend toward self-transformation. It was not Darwin, but some of his followers who concluded that this transformation necessarily carried along with it a sense of *progress*. Furthermore, even if we accept the metamorphosis of reptile into bird, this does not necessarily mean that reptiles will *disappear*, nor, for our purposes, does the fact that other activities emerge from the practice we know as Architecture and organize themselves as new disciplines

whatever can be most beautifully fitted out for the noble needs of man, by the movement of weights and the joining and massing of bodies," p. 3; Leon Battista Alberti, *L'architettura [De re aedificatoria]*, critical ed. Giovanni Orlandi, with intro and notes by Paolo Portoghesi, 2 vols. (Milan: Edizioni Il Polifilo, 1966), vol. 1, prologue, p. 2.

27 Kazys Varnelis, "One Thing After Another," *Log: Observations on Architecture and the Contemporary City* 3 (Fall 2004): 115; see also Iain Borden, "Death of Architecture," in *Hunch* 6/7 (Summer 2003): 105–110.

28 Kurt W. Forster, "Thoughts on the Metamorphoses of Architecture," *Log* 3 (Fall 2004): 19.

29 Ben van Berkel and Caroline Bos, "Weather, Wine, and Toenails," in *Hunch* 6/7 (Summer 2003): 90.

necessarily mean that Architecture as such will *disappear*. Witness the rise of fields like urbanism, industrial design, and countless other practices that at some point were included in the definition of Architecture. It is worth recalling that Alberti attributed the making of clocks to architects.

Furthermore, although Forster, Tafuri, and Hegel may not have been mistaken in their predictions of the disappearance of architecture *as we know it*, no one can assure us that we are on the eve of such a disappearance. For his part, Kenneth Frampton has proposed that "architecture can only survive as a form of critical culture, as a resistant 'otherness',"[30] but this demand for "resistance" is based on a somewhat nostalgic compulsion to extend the existence of a discipline that otherwise seems destined to disappear. It is appropriate, on the other hand, to ask what is the relationship of Architecture to that world which was so powerfully evoked by Marx, in which *"all that is solid melts into air"*? Guy Debord lucidly observed that: "Here we have the principle of commodity fetishism, the domination of society by things whose qualities are 'at the same time perceptible and imperceptible' by the senses. This principle is absolutely fulfilled in the spectacle, where the perceptible world is replaced by a set of images that are superior to that world yet at the same time impose themselves as *eminently* perceptible... Since the spectacle's job is to cause a world that is no longer directly perceptible to be *seen* via different specialized mediations, it is inevitable that it should elevate the human sense of sight to the special place once occupied by touch; the most abstract of the senses, and the most easily deceived, sight is naturally the most readily adaptable to present-day society's generalized abstraction."[31]

In this sense, Architecture, understood in absolutely traditional terms, seems still to be able to have the capacity to actively refute thet "melting into air," which, among many other things, carries along with it solidarity and empathy among human beings. And it does so with more efficacy than the presumed rebellion against, as Iain Borden asserts, "all institutional forms" which call for a "complete and permanent revolution, involving new forms of education, production, creativity, desires, self-management, territory."[32] Only a superficial approach to the practice of Richter & Dahl Rocha would identify its studied and profound archaism with a conservative attitude or an indifference to the world that surrounds it. Taking distance from currents and fashion, they obstinately pursue the work within Architecture as institution, in harmony with Adorno's idea of the role of the "sister" institution of Art. "For the disenchanted world, – stated Adorno – the fact of art is an outrage, an afterimage of enchantment, which it does not tolerate."[33]

*

30   Kenneth Frampton, "On the predicament of architecture at the end of the century," *Hunch* 6/7 (Summer 2003): 176.
31   Guy Debord, *The Society of the Spectacle*, trans. Donald Nicholson-Smith (New York: Zone Books, 1994), 26 and 17; originally published as *La Société du spectacle* (Paris: Editions Buchet-Chastel, 1967).
32   Iain Borden, "Death of architecture," p. 108.
33   Theodor Adorno, *Aesthetic Theory*, ed. Greta Adorno and Rolf Tiedemann, trans. and ed. with trans. intro. Robert Hullot-Kentor (Minneapolis: University of Minnesota Press, 1997), p. 58; originally published as *Aesthetische Theorie* (Berlin: Suhrkamp, 1970).

Archaism I: Character

The signature trait of Richter & Dahl Rocha's work is the legibility with which each project expresses the program for which it was conceived. Their building shapes do not belong to the universe of industrial, cybernetic, or biological form, nor are they purely geometric figures. There is no doubt about the function of the Route de Berne 46 office building, nor does the apartment building in Prilly-Lausanne reference anything but dwelling, while for the La Prairie Clinic at Montreux, the extension of its profile into the landscape, its terraces, and the asymmetry of its apertures work together to express with great lucidity a program that is about comfort and delight, not to mention efficiency. It is not difficult to recognize an educational purpose in the dimensions, siting, and materials selected for the Valmont Boarding School, nor is there anything obscure about the amenities offered by New Meeting Place on the campus of the Institute for Management Development (IMD) in Lausanne. In all of these cases, what is quietly revealed is the "character" of the architectural task, an ancient and specifically architectural way of affirming Aristotle's dictum that things (like the characters in his *Rhetoric*) are manifestly what they say they are.

Archaism II: Construction

Likewise, the works of Richter & Dahl Rocha are conceived with respect for their material condition. They are not mere "images," but tangible things. As such, they respond to the traditional function of architecture, that is, sheltering human activities. In order for this to happen, diverse elements that have weight, texture, gloss, color, and qualities such as waterproofing, heat resistance, and longevity must be assembled into a whole. The various tectonic, tactile, and visual properties of these elements are manipulated to produce sensations that amplify the specifically architectural discourse within which they interpret and respond to a given program. The red brick used in the residential development "Les Uttins" in Rolle highlights the ex-urban domestic condition of the project, while the black brick used for the rear facade of the residential complex "La Verrière" in Montreux resonates with the "hard" environment of the railroad tracks that abut the site. In all instances, these works exude the architects' pleasure, not so much in their material condition as the materiality of Architecture itself. In the same way, the wood of which the Forest Refuge is constructed palpably refers to the trees that surround it. Where there is a convergence between the density of craftsmanship, the consistency and precision of industrial materials, and the potential for invention, the *moderation* of Richter & Dahl Rocha's approach often produces a celebratory combination – for example, where glass is used in the form of bricks for the walls of the interior courtyard of "La Verrière" (either to cover or reveal in those suggestive "boxes" of light), as *brise-soleils* for UEFA's renovated Villa La Falaise, or as innovative signage for Nestlé. Given their avid engagement with the creative potential of the material world of building, it is not surprising that in a number of cases, Richter & Dahl Rocha's research into constructive solutions for a particular project has taken on a life of its own, resulting in reproducible products or systems. From a prototype for a Forest Refuge that can be constructed by rangers as needed, one at a time, to furniture developed for Nestlé Headquarters and later produced as a commercial line, a patented office partition system, and corporate signage that began as a unique solution and was later replicated, the firm's commitment to open-ended research and development ultimately inspired the founding of the affiliate firm, RDR Design.

Archaism III: Human Scale
When buildings are conceived as "spectacular" productions, remarkable artifice and ingenious invention occasionally conspire to elicit sensations that would be very much at home in an amusement park. This is not Richter & Dahl Rocha's goal. Instead, they closely attend to the richness of everyday life experiences. In striving to maintain dimensional relationships that refer to human scale, that of the user in whose service their projects are conceived and built, and with an eye to the "character" of the project, the architects pursue an approach that consists in searching for the most appropriate articulation of site and program. In their renovation of Nestlé Headquarters, the stately character of the glazed ground floor reception area is not a function of rigid composition or eye-catching materials, but rather the careful calibration of spatial relations in order to establish equilibrium between the interior space and the surrounding landscape. Richter & Dahl Rocha introduced a vertical plane of etched glass that acts as a screen behind the massive reception desk, proportioned in dynamic rapport with the dimensions of the gigantic hall. Against this freestanding translucent plane, the diminutive figure of a receptionist is gracefully framed by the immensity of the lakeside landscape. Attention to the issue of human scale is also evident in a very different case like the residential development Im Forster in Zurich, particularly in the solution proposed for the so-called *Mittelberg*. Here, the design consists of a small housing complex that presents itself not as a series but rather an ensemble of structures echoing the form of a single "grand mansion." Thus it manages to harmonize new and preexisting buildings. Richter & Dahl Rocha's project for Im Forster also effects a skillful artic-ulation of level changes in the terrain, in which structures only partially emerge from the earth in order not to dominate the magnificent park which belongs to the patrimony of that part of the city. A third and quite diverse example is the New Learning Center for IMD. Here again, the design is about inserting the work into a park setting, and in the context of a diverse group of buildings. The relationship between context and program required a differentiated morphology that would not overwhelm the natural setting. The appearance of the structure was reduced to an elevated volume supported by a powerful pair of arcades recalling Tschumi's approach. More than half of the functions are concealed below ground level. And, in this case, the curved skin of the emerging building is divided into semi-transparent panels the width of a forearm, which not only mediate the double-height of the building, but simultaneously reflect the surrounding trees.

Archaism IV: The Elements
Again and again, works of architecture must make use of the very elements of which they are composed. To provide shelter from sun and weather, builders developed inclined planes which came to be called roofs. To divide spaces, vertical elements called walls were introduced. To let air into enclosed spaces, builders invented the ingenious device of the window, and to change level, ramps, stairs, and mechani-cal devices. These were followed by sills, dormers, thresholds, parapets, ceilings, podiums, cornices, columns, and many other elements. While some architects have

tried to evade them, it is also possible to embrace the conventional elements of architecture as the continuously fascinating raw material of this ancient discipline. Richter & Dahl Rocha have taken a special interest in the transformative potential of such elements, which in their projects do not always function in expected ways. This is witnessed by the delicate stairs for their twin SWHome® villas at Chailly and the sculptural articulation of a stair linking two pre-existing structures that Richter & Dahl Rocha joined together for their Lausanne office. And in homage to Jean Tschumi's double-spiral Chambord stairway rising up through six floors of the original buildings, their own *pièce de résistance*, the Liaison Space, connects each floor of Tschumi's curvaceous structure with those of the simple bar building added in the 1970s. Given the unequal ceiling heights of the two buildings, ramps cutting through the atrium space fan out, floor to floor, to mediate the slight gaps. In a similar way, Richter & Dahl Rocha's projects explore a range of variations on the theme of the support, mediating the transition between the building and the ground. This has resulted in solutions as diverse as the series of concrete pilotis at street level supporting the residential complex "La Verrière," whose site rises up sharply behind it to carry the railroad tracks, and those of the office building at Route de Berne 46, essentially square or rectangular pilotis, or abstract prisms, supports that reflect their material aspect, such as the Richter & Dahl Rocha Office, or cylindrical pilotis, like those used in the La Prairie Clinic. In other instances, the architects have arrived at more sophisticated solutions, such as the sculptural arcades of the New Learning Center for IMD, the complex system of supports for the Nestlé restaurant, the slender, decorated columns for the New Meeting Place on the IMD campus, and even, in a totally opposite extreme, the gigantic blocks that support the New Museum of Fine Arts in Lausanne. The works of Richter & Dahl Rocha do not emerge from the ground, nor do they try to float above it: As is natural in Architecture, they simply rest on it. And often, in order to do this, they employ that element of transition between building and ground called the podium. Sometimes it is the plane that supports a group of buildings, as in the residential development "La Verrière." On other occasions, it is the building itself that unfolds into the surrounding terrain, as with the supporting walls of the La Prairie Clinic extension, or defines a terrace, like the New Meeting Place for IMD, or contains part of the building – as also happens with the project for Route de Berne 46. Even an edge beam can become a podium, as evidenced in the Swiss National Train Maintenance Center in Geneva, and likewise, the concrete cylinders that articulate such a transition in the modest Forest Refuge.

Archaism V: Context
In their practice, Richter & Dahl Rocha concentrate on the making of architecture, attending as precisely as possible to the requirements of their clients, whether public or private, but always taking extreme care with their handling of whatever portion of the natural or built environment their projects occupy. In this sense, context is of paramount concern. A project like their residential complex "La Verrière," for example, is as strongly determined by the structures that surround it as it is conditioned by the massive infrastructure of the railroad passing directly behind it. Facing the lake, it confronts the historic Montreux Palace Hotel, but the architects have also taken into account the character of all the lesser important

buildings along this street. On the other hand, with their extension of the La Prairie Clinic, the architects kept the structures low, with three floors semi-buried in the ground to emphasize the volume of the existing "Chateau" and the Shalom Villa at the upper end of the site. But as it unfolds into terraces, it also follows the slope of the site, making reference to the local vineyards. In the same way, the dramatic horizontality of the Nestlé Product Technology Center in Singen, Germany, heightens the presence of the building, while at the same time deftly integrating it into the nondescript industrial context with brick cladding and calibrating its height to that of the surrounding structures. The five-story Route de Berne 46 office building, located in a suburban neighborhod comprised of low buildings, could have dominated its context. To avoid this effect, the building volume was subdivided so that the ground floor and mezzanine appear to rest on a second plane, and the three upper floors were treated as a unified piece made to seem "lighter" by the movement of louver-like *brise-soleil* elements, reducing its overall impact. In the same regard, it seems appropriate to consider how Richter & Dahl Rocha's buildings for IMD and the residential development for Im Forster are articulated in their park-like settings, and also how the Valmont Boarding School in a quiet residential neighborhod achieves harmony with its context by reducing the large volume of the gymnasium to a minimal height which gently communicates with the houses that surround it.

✳

The Role of Technique

The only possible legitimacy for the modern work of art comes from within, from its potential to be "autonomous." This necessity for autonomy is absolute, that is, the totality of the work's component parts must be subsumed to it. However, the work of architecture presents problems of a greater complexity than other artistic endeavors, given that its autonomy must mediate incalculable factors such as the use of a building or the strength of materials used to build it. For Adorno, within the modern work of art there is a struggle between nature, to whose own determinations the structure of materials that comprise the work must be assimilated, and the modernist mandate for the autonomy of form. Adorno rightly maintains that it is inevitable that, "in the impulse of every particular element of art works toward integration, the disintegrative impulse of nature secretly manifests itself. The more integrated artworks are, the more what constitutes them disintegrates in them. To this extent their success is their decomposition and that lends them their fathomlessness."[34]

But this written-in-stone law about the necessity for form to triumph over materials in the condition of modernity produces a profound disorientation, to the extent that modernity does not provide any basis for or indication about the organization of form. Therefore, and in the particular case of architecture, it is customary to make use of consoling alternatives such as the supposed "objectivity" of functionalism, postmodernist irresponsibility, atemporal typological categories, and geometrization. However, the most lasting consolation is that of *technique*.

34 Adorno, *Aesthetic Theory*, p. 52.

The organization of form based on the logic of technology – whether with respect to process, mimesis of the formal-mechanical universe, or materials – carries two additional reassurances: alignment with the course of progress, and the supposed approximation of truth. Adorno observed that "the technologization of art is no less provoked by the subject – by the disillusioned consciousness and the mistrust of magic as a veil – than by the object: by the problem of how artworks may be bindingly organized. The possibility of the latter became problematic with the collapse of traditional procedures, however much of their influence has extended into the current epoch. Only technology provided a solution; it promised to organize art completely in terms of that means-end relation that Kant had in general equated with the aesthetic."[35]

The link between technical "progress" and the human condition has been amply explored (not to mention cast into question) by philosophy itself, and this is not the place to pursue the issue. However, with respect to the work of Richter & Dahl Rocha, it may be productive to consider the relationship between technique and "truth." This relationship was at the center of architectural debates during the 1950s and 1960s, when "Brutalism" was fiercely articulated in connection with the existentialist demand for "authenticity." Behind these positions, the phantom of Ruskin and 19th-century organicism lurked, along with a latent devotion to the notion of a mimetic relationship between architecture and nature. Beyond the artifices (academic in the 19th century and "aesthetic" or ideological in the early 20th century) architects would make it their mission to reveal the (natural) truth through the materiality of architecture. The modernist destruction of the moorings of "truth" beyond the scope of representation was countered with the belief in its unmediated presence in the transparent articulation of materials, in response to a logic of technique presumed to be "pure." Architecture, understood as institution, entails, on the contrary, a clear consciousness of the conventional basis for "truth." And the modern condition with its demand for the subordination of material/nature to the autonomy of form only reinforces that artificial condition as superfluous, as valid only in the domain of the representation of "truth."

In one of his most convincing works,[36] Gianni Vattimo has developed this idea of constructed truth within the context of a certain order of representations in Nietzsche's work on the "mask." Vattimo demonstrates that for Nietzsche, "in the second Untimely Meditation, beyond the disguise of the decadent man that cannot take the initiative and dons a mask of stereotypical roles, 'masks with only one expression', we encounter a masking that is not only not connected with decadence, but on the contrary seems to be the only means of avoiding it: the definition and delimiting of the boundaries of a horizon of historical action which demands assuming some element of the historical being as 'value'."[37] Following Nietzsche's lucid vision, the masking is not disguise or mediation (as in representations), but presents itself as the inevitable mode of human construction of the world. Precisely for that reason, Vattimo reminds us that "in the second Untimely Meditation, the overcoming of the decline of historicist civilization should come about by virtue of

35 Ibid., p. 59.
36 Gianni Vattimo, *Il soggetto e la maschera: Nietzsche e il problema della liberazione* (Milan: Bompiano, 1974).
37 Vattimo, *Il soggetto e la maschera*, p. 23 (our translation).

'everlasting forces' such as art and religion, which are not at all ways of disguising true reality, but 'masks' in themselves, illusions, fictions. Civilization taken to be the model, the 'classic', is not contrary to decline as the world of the true, but rather eminently the world of fiction and mask. In spite of the fact that all of this raises some difficulties, it does not allow Nietzsche's discourse to be reduced simply to the distinction between a civilization of becoming, and therefore no fiction, and another where – because of the lack of creative forces – man disguises himself. Also, the first of these civilizations is a creation of masks, illusions and fictions. They are so in spite of confronting disguise, precisely because – in opposition to disguise – they do not want to be confused with reality; and they even disclose 'reality' itself in its guise of appearance, of a mask that does not want to be seen as such."[38] At this point, any intent to "disclose" the supposed truth through the Brutalist demonstration of the technical roots of building not only results in a futile demonstration, but almost a century and a half after the Nietzschean enlightenment, also seems pathetic. In the practice of Richter & Dahl Rocha, technique occupies, on the other hand, the same subordinate space that it occupied in the traditional practice of architecture, even setting aside the illusion of tectonics. Marco De Michelis reminds us that "the term *tectonic* was coined at the beginning of the 19th century as an instrument for reconstituting the lost unity of the architectonic organism by the combination and juxtaposition of building elements."[39] In the architecture of Richter & Dahl Rocha, on the other hand, the unity does not respond to the logic of such juxtapositions, and very often negates it.

In their residential project "Les Uttins," for example, the slabs of one of the main facades of the building seem to be suspended without any support, while on the rear facade, the brick wall (which seems at first sight to be a supporting wall) is fenestrated irregularly, making it difficult to understand its structural logic. With the La Prairie Clinic, the podium of the building is comprised of stonework like that used to retain the terraced vineyard slopes characteristic of the region around Montreux. However, instead of reinforcing its condition of weight (represented by the small windows), at the lower level, the building opens up in its full extension with the glass facade of a restaurant that belongs to a last band of material – clear and abstract – presenting the tectonic artifice of the bands of "stone." Furthermore, the presumably "rustic" condition of that same "stone" presents itself as a "mask" by showing the polished sides made visible as doorjambs. In the same way, in the center of the Nestlé Product Technology Centre at Singen, the facades of the building not only enunciate the condition of "extension" inherent in the building's structure, but also present themselves as two distinctly different "faces." The brick used on one of the facades is suspended over the continuous windows, and clearly "applied," as is revealed by the metal frames that support it. The lateral ends, on the other hand, are signs that literally indicate the function of the building. The roof of the New Meeting Place on the IMD campus in Lausanne is supported by off-center columns of the interior, while on the exterior, this tectonic logic is neither revealed nor is it completely disguised. It "tells" us that the

38   Ibid., p. 40 (our translation).
39   Marco De Michelis, "Morphing Metamorph," *Log: Observations on Architecture and the Contemporary City* 4 (Winter 2005): 10.

horizontal plane which encloses it is supported by the robust wooden vertical elements that act as *brise-soleils*.

The Swiss National Train Maintenance Center in Geneva is another telling example of the "double play" in which Richter & Dahl Rocha are engaged in relation to technical issues. On the one hand such issues are not denied, as with contemporary practice in thrall to a dominant geometrization, the "white cubes" of the first modernists, or architecture subordinated to formalist decisions, but neither do Richter & Dahl Rocha pretend that technique is the dominant parameter. It is quite evident that the distribution of "loads" in this industrial project does not follow the logic of its supports. On the contrary, the aluminum facing appears to hover lightly above, while the dark wood panel seems to be unsupported weight. This is because, in its full extension, the continuous window offers open vistas to the exterior for the workers inside. Nothing of the engineered structure of the building is expressed in its architecture. The elements that comprise this enclosure mask the interior space without pretending that it expresses its unity on the exterior. On the contrary, on the exterior there is a three-fold partition that does not exist in the interior. The materials work in opposition to one another, in such a way that the polished, clear, and reflective metallic surface of the roof is opposed to the rough, dark, and opaque surface of the wood. The latter is obviously the predominant element for the image of the building. It does not declare its materiality directly, but rather through a metaphoric process. Like the tragic or comic gestures on the masks worn by characters in the classical theatre, the rustic quality of the wooden blocks speak to us as they refer to, or "represent" the arduous, mechanical, and to a certain extent, primary condition of the manual labor going on inside.

✳

Past, Present, Future

Hannah Arendt has proposed the need to distinguish between the human "condition" and "nature," and insists that "human nature" entails the search for an essence, for the being of humans, and thus inevitably leads toward metaphysics, and ultimately, divinity. To avoid this path without necessarily attempting to deny it, the disciple of Heidegger and Husserl prefers to speak of specific conditions of the human. Following a Marxist tradition, albeit in a critical mode, Arendt recognizes among the most important of these conditions the capacity to work, to produce world, as distinct from labor which is the activity destined to reproduce the natural condition of life. To produce world is to produce objects that are not condemned to pass fleetingly through human existence only to return immediately to nature, such as with food, for example. To produce world is, according to Arendt, to produce objects that resist immediate consumption, and thus to resist time, to produce objects whose value resides precisely in the fact that they last even beyond the lifetime of the individuals who generated them. "It is indeed the mark of all laboring," she wrote, "that it leaves nothing behind, that the result of its effort is almost as quickly consumed as the effort is spent.... Insofar as the intellectual is indeed not a 'worker' – who like all other workers, from the humblest craftsman to the greatest artist, is engaged in adding one more, if possible durable, thing to the human artifice – he resembles perhaps nobody so much as Adam Smith's 'menial servant', although his function is less to keep the life process intact and provide for its regeneration than to care for the upkeep of the various gigantic bureaucratic machines whose processes consume their services and devour their products as quickly and mercilessly as the biological life process itself.... The products of work – and not the products of labor – guarantee the permanence and durability without which a world would not be possible at all."[40] This distinction with respect to the role of work as a mode of constructing world in time and throughout time, is reinforced in an observation by Walter Benjamin in the same vein. In his *Theses on the Philosophy of History*, Benjamin wrote that "our image of happiness is indissolubly bound up with the image of redemption.... There is a secret agreement between past generations and the present one. Our coming was expected on earth. Like every generation that preceded us, we have been endowed with a weak Messianic power, a power to which the past has a claim....[41] The class struggle... is a fight for the crude and material things without which no refined and spiritual things could exist.... They manifest themselves in this struggle as courage, humor, cunning, and fortitude. They have retroactive force and will constantly call in question every victory, past and present.... As the flowers turn toward the sun, by dint of a secret heliotropism the past strives to turn toward the sun which is rising in the sky of history."[42]

Therefore, without work there can be neither duration nor time, because the instant consumption of the products of labor implies that human life remains trapped in the timeless cyclical flux of the voracious movement of nature towards its final stasis. Works of architecture are for society like the table or family vase, like the beloved pencil or the old sweater, like all the things and beings that accompany us and help us understand our own unity as individuals in spite of our perpetual transformation. Without those fixed points, without those imprints of human work, society is adrift in the timeless eternity of nature. Without those common possessions that we receive and leave behind as our heritage, the individuals that make up a generation lose the threads that unite them and by the force of entropy tend to be transformed into autonomous particles who even lose sight of their own human condition.

I believe that the work of Richter & Dahl Rocha belongs to those architectures understood to be foundational for the constitution of our world, as a privileged medium for the preservation of human sociability and historicity. Given the demand for immediate consumption and the general instability of the modern metropolitan condition, in addition to the acceleration of the process of dispersal of all values as a result of the unstoppable force of globalization, the capacity for resistance is under

40 Hannah Arendt, *The Human Condition* (Chicago: University of Chicago Press, 1993; 1st edition, 1958). "The reality and reliability of the human world rest primarily on the fact that we are surrounded by things more permanent than the activity by which they were produced, and potentially even more permanent than the lives of their authors. Human life, in so far as it is world-building, is engaged in a constant process of reification, and the degree of worldliness of produced things, which all together form the human artifice, depends upon their greater or lesser permanence in the world itself."
41 Walter Benjamin, "Theses on the Philosophy of History," in *Illuminations: Essays and Reflections*, ed. Hannah Arendt (New York: Schocken Books, 1968), Thesis II, p. 253; "Über den Begriff der Geschichte," completed in spring 1940, was first published in *Die neue Rundschau* 61/3 (1950).
42 pp. 254f.

siege, and, I would venture to say, along with it, the essence of the discipline of architecture. The vindication for architecture in the traditional institutional sense comes about because of the need to introduce within our conception of this activity the temporal role – what Mishima calls the vessel of time – which the discipline must assume. The institution of architecture entails, among other things, the possibility of receiving that "endowment" mentioned by Benjamin, introducing to it the traces of our own existence and bequeathing it once again to future generations. This transmission is impossible without common codes, although – like language – these can (and should) always be modified.

Adolf Loos pointed to the crux of this problem in his essay "Ornament and Crime."[43] For Loos, because of the terms of its production, architecture could not easily assimilate itself to the processes of other commodities of more transitory utility. Following Boullé, the architect of the Michaelerplatz house believed that, to ensure that the exterior of a luxurious coat or a work of architecture would maintain its cultural relevance for the maximum length of time (that its use value would endure), the exterior had to possess a "resistant form" with respect to the passage of time. Assuming architecture to be an example of *Formermüdung*, or "resistant form," Loos questioned the supposed absence of limits in the universal process of homogenization ensured by the market. To enter into the problem of time, and with it the need for "resistant form," invokes the need to work within architecture as "institution," that is, as the space of a social contract.

This is why an "institutional" practice such as that of Richter & Dahl Rocha can neither ignore the problem of its possible permanence ("turn towards the sun") and limit itself to a pure present nor settle its account with history. It is this situation that enables the work to establish a dialogue with the masterworks of the past. In the West at least, these comprise a particular type of solution that facilitates transgenerational dialogue. Every creator, according to the polemical literary critic Harold Bloom, struggles to reach the level of the masterworks that preceded him or her, and only in reaching them can he or she consider a new opportunity: "There can be no strong, canonical writing without the process of literary influence, a process vexing to undergo and difficult to understand.... The anxiety of influence is not an anxiety about the father, real or literary, but an anxiety achieved by and in the poem, novel or play. Any strong literary work creatively misreads and therefore misinterprets a precursor text. An authentic canonical writer may or may not internalize her or his work's anxiety, but that scarcely matters: the strongly achieved work is the anxiety.... Tradition is not only a handing–down or process of benign transmission; it is also a conflict between past genius and present aspiration, in which the prize is literary survival or canonical inclusion."[44]

That trans-generational dialogue, as well as the impact of the relationship be-tween past and future on contemporary creative work is manifest in Richter & Dahl Rocha's production. That preoccupation undoubtedly made an early appearance with Jacques Richter's interest in the Tendenza group, whereas in the case of

43   Adolf Loos, "Ornament and Crime," published in *Ornament and Crime: Selected Essays*, intro. Adolf Opel, trans. Michael Mitchell (Riverside, Calif.: Ariadne Press, 1998); originally trans. from German and ed. Marcel Ray, *Les cahiers d'aujourdhui* 5 (1913): 247–256.
44   Harold Bloom, *The Western Canon: The Books and School of the Ages* (New York: Harcourt Brace, 1994), p. 8.

Dahl Rocha, it was already apparent in his house in San Isidro, with its explicit references to Loos's *Raumplan*, the Mies of the Krefeld houses, and Argentine precedents such as that of Carlos Vilar. But that same preoccupation has been maturing in the universe of Richter & Dahl Rocha's recent work. Think, for example, of their inspired handling of apparently commonplace elements such as the *brise-soleils* designed for the office building at Route de Berne 46. The vertical elements that cover main facade may *seem* to repeat an inherited solution, one that has been applied in countless instances since Le Corbusier, and which the Brazilian architects developed in the early modern period. But in the hands of Richter & Dahl Rocha, this inheritance is inflected with an almost imperceptible variation: a small glass louver-like element that controls and filters light entering the building. The New Meeting Place on the IMD campus stands as another example of this open dialogue with the past. The existing structures on the campus did not dictate the scheme for the underlying structure that organizes the new building, but it moves carefully within the dimensions of the courtyard, establishes a continuity with the existing cornice, and engages it in conversation through the use of brick pillars on the angle evoking those that frame the original piece. Furthermore, Richter & Dahl Rocha's building does not strive for absolute novelty. In the elegant play between slender vertical elements and overhanging planes, it invokes the American Prairie School and its Californian successors of the 1940s, while echoing Oscar Niemeyer and Lúcio Costa's Brazilian pavilion for the 1939 New York World's Fair.

Perhaps most forceful of all is the example of Richter & Dahl Rocha's transformation of Jean Tschumi's 1958 Nestlé Headquarters. Here, history, and thus time, was the central problem. Considered of the best examples of modern architecture in Switzerland, the building was in dire need of updating, considering the fact that it is, so to speak, "alive" and the "aura" of the existing structure in addition to its landmark status demanded an extremely careful approach. The result, in spite of the functional and technical transformations geared to preserving the original appearance and facilitating its ongoing function as headquarters for a multinational corporation, offers not only a completely new reading of the original project and the 1970s addition (here, the role of the new circulation plan was decisive), but also incorporates into the building's legacy entirely new dimensions and absolutely novel moments. Richter & Dahl Rocha's design for the new Museum of Fine Arts in Lausanne (2004–05), with its pure volume suspended in space by minimal supports, invokes a history that runs the gamut from the adventurous experiments of the Russian constructivists to the systematic efforts of Mies van der Rohe. However, that is not to overlook the impact of Lina Bo Bardi's Art Museum in São Paulo, itself rooted in outstanding precedents like Niemeyer's museum in Brasilia, and some recent works by Paulo Mendes da Rocha, for example. Going much further back in terms of references, Richter & Dahl Rocha's modest Forest Refuge stands as a sensitive reflection of continuities and breaks with the house/home as the basic unit of shelter. From its source in the mythical-universal form of the primeval hut to an ingenious rethinking of the double-gabled roof and rotated floor plan, their prototypical dwelling unit looks as far backward as it looks forward.

✳

*...und Aschenbach empfand wie schon oftmals mit Schmerzen, daß das Wort
die sinnliche Schönheit nur zu preisen, nicht wiederzugeben vermag.*
Thomas Mann, *Death in Venice* (1908)[45]

*Bello es una palabra revolucionaria. Tiene que ver con las emociones, con la atracción, pero también con la
búsqueda y la investigación. Herbert Marcuse ha escrito sobre este aspecto revolucionaro de la belleza.*
Jacques Herzog[46]

The Principle of Hope

For those who are able to refuse the demand for spectacularity required by immediate consumption, and who are able to give themselves the necessary time to enjoy it, Richter & Dahl Rocha's architecture thrills, in intense and unique ways. But that intensity works upon our senses in the register of *pianissimo*, an almost inaudible whisper, in stark contrast to the "shock," the provocative shriek of the metropolitan *Nervenleben*. If one contemplates the work very attentively, it is possible to perceive the subtle resonance that signals the ontological difference between architecture and construction.

In his essay on Max Bill, Von Moos declared the architecture of the Swiss master to have been "an architecture devoid of utopian sentiment."[47] If we consider that utopia can only be expressed through the direct presentation of programs and/or forms conceived exclusively within the context of a future social or cultural formation, his assertion would be sound. But if we understand utopia as a nonexistent place, where the unattainable aspirations of the present can be expressed, then it is unfair to deny this dimension of Bill's architecture. The observation may, or rather should be extended to the appreciation of Richter & Dahl Rocha's work, particularly in the terms set forth by Ernest Bloch in *The Principle of Hope*,[48] where utopia contained within the most intense works of art does not reside in its explicit discourse, in its content, but in its ability to constitute itself as a source of hope. And precisely, following Baudelaire's prescient definition of modernity, beauty is above all – as Baudelaire would take delight in paraphrasing Stendhal – the *promise of happiness*. In his review of *The Principle of Hope*, Roland Aronson framed Bloch's position in this way: "[for Bloch] to hope, most simply put, is to anticipate a better world in the future – the 'still unbecome, still unachieved homeland' – and to act to create that world, based on real tendencies in the present."[49] Aronson further asserted that Bloch's project was in a sense a reaction to the fact that "philosophy has ignored the future, and thus has lacked the tools for discerning how the utopian function operates in the 'nearest nearness'

---

45   *Death in Venice*, trans. Kenneth Burke (New York: Knopf, 1965), p. 76: "...and Aschenbach was distressed, as he had often been before, by the thought that words can only exalt sensuous beauty, not give it back" (our emendation of the translation); Thomas Mann, *Der Tod in Venedig, Romane und Erzählungen* (Berlin & Weimar: Aufbau-Verlag, 1975), p. 518; first published as *Der Tod in Venedig: Novelle* (Munich: Hyperion, 1912); .
46   "Finos arquitectos constructores," interview with Jacques Herzog by Fredy Massad and Alicia Guerrero Yeste, *Summa+* 35 (February-March 1999): 112: "Beauty is a revolutionary word. It has to do with emotions, with attraction, but also with searching and investigation. Herbert Marcuse has written about this revolutionary aspect of beauty" (our translation).
47   Von Moos, "Max Bill. A la búsqueda de la 'cabaña primitiva'," p. 17.
48   Ernst Bloch, *The Principle of Hope*, trans. Neville Plaice, Stephen Plaice, and Paul Knight (Cambridge, Mass.: The MIT Press, 1986).
49   Ronald Aronson, "Ernst Bloch, *The Principle of Hope*" (Review Essay) *History & Theory* 30/2 (May 1991): 226 (quoting from Bloch, *The Principle of Hope*, p. 9).

of the present. But artistic genius grasps, and presents, material that is beyond 'what has previously been consciously given, what has previously been explicated and finally formed the world'."[50] "'Every great work of art this still remains, except for its manifest character, impelled towards the latency of the other side, i.e., towards the contents of a future which had not yet appeared in its own time'."[51]

The significance of Baudelaire's "In Praise of Make-up" (1863) for understanding the depth of the issue of beauty has been pointed out by Franco Rella,[52] who identifies what he calls the *enigma* of beauty, or the search for beauty as dissatisfaction. "The beautiful is also supernatural, and ornament, *la parure*, cosmetics, demonstrate 'a disgust' for that which simply is, and they express in this way a metaphysical anguish."[53] And paraphrasing Baudelaire, he continues describing those ephemeral adornments as "a new effort, more or less accomplished, towards the beautiful, any approximation towards an ideal, whose desire the unsatisfied human spirit relentlessly seeks."[54]

To emphasize the point: the hope Bloch talks about is not limited to a purely metaphysical dimension. "In this view hope becomes a discourse of critique and social transformation. Hope makes the leap for us between critical education, which tells us what must be changed; political agency, which gives us the means to make change; and the concrete struggles through which change happens. Hope, in short, gives substance to the recognition that every present is incomplete. For theorists such as Bloch (Lerner, West and Kelley), hope is anticipatory rather than messianic, mobilizing rather than therapeutic. Understood in this way, the longing for a more humane society does not collapse into a retreat from the world but becomes a means to engage with present behaviors, institutional formations, and everyday practice. Hope in this context does not ignore the worst dimensions of human suffering, exploitation, and social relations; on the contrary.... it acknowledges the need to sustain the 'capacity to see the worst and offer more than that for our consideration'."[55] In my judgment, through its commitment to the search for beauty, Architecture responds – in its central demand – to the construction of such hope. The work of Richter & Dahl Rocha, the varied aspects that unfold within it, come together around this idea. There is no cohesive force other than the search for beauty, which articulates the complex layers of demand, aspiration, and meaning that comprise it.

In the first place, this is a response to the chaos and ugliness of the contemporary metropolitan condition. We perceive this as the absolute absence of form, or at least as the tendency toward the dissolution of boundaries and the comprehensible structure of the traditional city. If the city's reason for being consists in its capacity to

50 Ibid. (quoting from Bloch, *The Principle of Hope*, p. 126).
51 Ibid. (quoting from Bloch, *The Principle of Hope*, p. 127).
52 Franco Rella; "Elogio della bellezza," Franco Rella, ed., *Forme e Pensiero del Moderno* (Milan: Feltrinelli, 1989), p. 84 (our translation): *"Anche il bello è sovrannaturale, e l'ornamento, la parure, il maquillage, dimostrano "un disgusto" per ciò che semplicemente è, ed esprimono così un'ansia metafisica; see also Belleza e verità, ed.* Franco Rella (Milan: Feltrinelli, 1990), and *L'enigma della bellezza* (Milan: Feltrinelli, 1991).
53 Rella, "Elogio della bellezza, p. 84.
54 Ibid.: *"uno sforzo nuovo, più o meno felice verso il bello, una approssimazione qualsiasi verso un ideale, il cui desiderio sollecita senza pòsa lo spirito umano insodisfatto."*
55 Henry Giroux, "When Hope is Subversive," *Tikkun* 19/6 (November-December 2004): 63.

engender a common social project, then the contemporary hypermetropolis, on the other hand, is the non-place where all social connections are broken. And, if to restore them the project entails the constitution of a recognizable urban unity, its absence in the hypermetropolitan condition generates in its inhabitants total freedom and at the same time, total and distressing loneliness.

However, the dissatisfaction with *beauty* is not produced by its lack as much as by what it contains that is inaccessible to us, by its over-determination. So impossible to apprehend is the beautiful that in spite of the fact that it is apparently codifiable, given that it does not reduce itself to subjective impressions, all attempts to reproduce it strictly through its codes are doomed to fail. And works produced in this manner are almost always born with the appearance of death. As I have discussed elsewhere,[56] in its completeness, *beauty* constitutes itself, in this sense, as denunciation, because by virtue of being uniquely localized and identified it illuminates its absence beyond its limits. In the context of the contemporary hypermetropolis, and particularly in the case of its most underdeveloped expressions, beauty makes ugliness even more striking and inadmissible, as Marc Cousins has formulated it.[57] It is the possibility of the beautiful, the hope for beauty that urges us to avoid the inhumanity of ugliness. Or, in Adorno's words: "Art must take up the case of what is proscribed as ugly, though no longer in order to integrate or mitigate it or to reconcile it with its own existence through humor that is more offensive than anything repulsive. Rather, in the ugly, art must denounce the world that creates and reproduces the ugly in its own image, even if in this too the possibility persists that sympathy with the degraded will reverse into concurrence with degradation."[58]

Rem Koolhaas, who has launched a lucid critique of those who invoke the ancient concept of mimesis in a superficial manner, proposed the analogy: "You are in a mess, we are in a mess, you are unstructured, we are unstructured, you are vulgar, we are vulgar, you are chaotic, we are chaotic.... The only relationship that architects can have with chaos is by taking their rightful place in the army of those committed to prevent it, and fail."[59] The demand for beauty that architecture proposes to us must be read in this first sense, as a critique of the rhizomatic expansion of fragments of urbanity without scale, boundaries, or articulation. And in opposition to that expansion, not with a totalitarian gesture that pretends to the original *One*, no less fragmentary a fragmentary action, which, conscious of its own impotence, proposes those crystallizations that like all forms of life are impulses in opposition to entropy.

Following Augustine, for Simone Weil, "The first of the soul's needs, the one which touches most nearly its eternal destiny, is order, that is to say, a texture of social relationships such that no one is compelled to violate imperative obligations.... We love the beauty of the world, because we sense behind it the presence of something akin to that wisdom we should like to possess to slake our thirst for

56   Jorge F. Liernur, "Toward a Disembodied Architectural culture," *Anybody*, ed. Cynthia Davidson (New York: Any Corporation, 1997), p. 196.
57   Marc Cousins, "The Ugly," in *AA Files* 28 (1995): 3–6.
58   Adorno, *Aesthetic Theory*, p. 48.
59   Rem Koolhaas, in "Finding Freedoms: Conversations with Rem Koolhaas," by Alejandro Zaera Polo, *El Croquis* 53 (1992): 16 and 27.

good. In a minor degree, really beautiful works of art are examples of 'ensembles' in which independent factors concur, in a manner impossible to understand, so as to form a unique thing of beauty."[60] At the origin of the conception of the beautiful in the West, in his *Poetics*, Aristotle conceives of it precisely in this register, confronted with the abyss of a formless and incomprehensible universe: "A beautiful object, whether it be a living organism or any whole composed of parts must not only have an orderly arrangement of parts, but must also be of a certain magnitude; for beauty depends on magnitude and order."[61] Furthermore, Aristotle claims that *social beauty* depends on the correct relationship between the number of inhabitants and the size of the city.[62] But the demand for beauty may have another reading in terms of the social. The cohesion, boundary, and order required by Aristotle had already been described by pre-Socratic philosophers such as Heraclitus and Pythagoras as *harmony*.[63] Harmony is, above all, *assemblage*, the condition of reunion of parts. And, underlying the appearance, what determines that assemblage of things, the totality of things, is a network of relationships that are established among all of relationships in the universe. The basis for those relationships is established by the number or amount, and because of this, the relationship between the object and the world is an inextricable aspect of the condition of the beautiful as it has been constructed historically.

Different from the perception of that which is pleasant to the senses, that which belongs to the subjective realm of the aesthetic, *beauty* only exists in the social dimension of the human condition. Hans-Georg Gadamer writes: "Despite this, the kind of truth that we encounter in the experience of the beautiful does unambiguously make a claim to more than merely subjective validity. Otherwise it would have no binding truth for us. When I find something beautiful, I do not simply mean that it pleases me in the same sense that I find a meal to my taste. When I find something beautiful, I think that it 'is' beautiful. Or, to adapt a Kantian expression, 'I demand everyone's agreement'."[64]

The claim for the *beautiful* is therefore an attempt to overcome the individualistic and subjective regression, both at the merely aesthetic level, and also on the level of the not necessarily shared enlightenment of the artistic. One condition for the existence of *beauty* is, in other words, the condition of its articulation – as a category – within a global cultural construction. It is true that the work of art does not link or reduce itself to the idea of the beautiful; and, furthermore, the authoritarian temptation that underlies the concept of beauty itself cannot be ignored. But precisely for that reason, to make it productive, we must understand it as a paradox, as an open problem. In referring to the ontological characteristics of commodities, Gadamer has written that "it is fitting, therefore, that the only "things" we know are mass-produced in factories, marketed with intensive advertising, and finally thrown away when they are broken. They cannot help us

60 Simone Weil, *The Need for Roots: Prelude to a Declaration of Duties Toward Mankind*, intro. T. S. Eliot, trans. Arthur Wills (New York & London: Routledge, 2002), pp. 10f.
61 Aristotle, *Poetics*, quoted in Ernesto Grassi, *Die Theorie des Schönen in der Antike* (Cologne: Dumont, 1980), p. 183.
62 Aristotle, *Politics*; quoted in Grassi, *Die Theorie des Schönen in der Antike*, p. 184.
63 See Jan Patothcka, *L'Art et le Temps* (Vienna: Presses Pocket/P.O.L., 1992).
64 Hans-Georg Gadamer; "Art and Imitation," *The Relevance of the Beautiful and Other Essays*, trans. Nicholas Walker (Cambridge: Cambridge University Press, 1986), pp. 102f.

to experience what things are. Through them we are unable to experience the presence of what is essentially irreplaceable, there is nothing historical about them and they have no life."[65]

For this reason, in the current condition of one-dimensional homogenization and of reproducibility, the *beautiful* constitutes itself as an impregnable core. Everything can be consumed, and particularly prone to that risk are the artistic expressions that present themselves as virulent and contingent negations of the existing. Because as such, they feed the series of infinite replacements required by the machinery of capitalist production. In that machinery, the abominable but inevitable destiny of the avant-garde is publicity. *Beauty* confronts that consumability because the agreement, the human reunion it is based on, beyond subjective sensations, does not have the limit of the present moment, nor even those of its own time. We would not ask ourselves about beauty if we did not receive perplexing traces of its experience in other generations, and even other geographies. If the work of Richter & Dahl Rocha can be faulted, it would be on account of its beauty. In it we perceive the powerful will of "reunion," of "order," of "harmony," of "balance," of "proportion," of "stability," of "atemporality," of "restraint," of "gracefulness," of "elegance," of "certainty," and of "consistency," that characterize works we call beautiful. Of course these are insignificant attributes for an important part of contemporary critique, but what for some constitutes a demerit, becomes for the rest of us a rare and necessary virtue.

All of the work done for the renovation of Nestlé Headquarters, one of the best examples of this virtue, attests to Richter & Dahl Rocha's powerful commitment to the orchestration of the parts of a whole whose unity has been challenged by previous interventions – even their interventions in the typical floor plan, which were directed to the subtle highlighting of an intent not fully realized in Tschumi's original building . Echoing the grand Chambord staircase and the entrance canopy, referencing the formal allusions of the floor plan, reinterpreting with new materials and diverse morphologies the magnificent columns of the arcade of the Tschumi building, the new Nestlé restaurant constitutes a moment of great intensity. Probably inherited from this strong referent, the curves of ample radius were rehearsed for the first time in the Prilly-Lausanne building complex, becoming dominant in the La Prairie Clinic extension. Here they act as a device to connect an extremely complex and diverse group of pre-existing buildings. La Prairie also accounts for the attention given to light as a modeling and organizing matter of the work. The main function of the clinic, the care of the body, calls for light that has a soft presence appearing from unexpected sources or filtered through control systems.

The synecdoche, or the careful relationship of the parts to the whole, is another of the conditions for achieving beauty. The way this materializes in Richter & Dahl Rocha's "Les Uttins" development reminds us of the fantastic work by Bruno Taut in Britz. The building group is defined by a series of variations on a typology which all refer to one another. When the building is facing the landscape as the main determining event, the pieces are capable of disappearing as autonomous

65 Ibid.

elements, and giving way to the totality, to their presentation as a whole, through the flow from one end to the other of the mezzanine floors. But to this unified reading, others are added. To begin with, the several blocks comprising the site. From this position it is possible to read the double-front terraces as bridges between the units, which are identified as independent brick volumes. Finally, it is also clear that those blocks allow units that are independent of one another to form a unit, with unique characteristics as is clearly expressed by the irregular rhythm of the apertures.

There is no beauty without a clear determination of the boundaries of the work. These may be established by a formal structure with an interior centrality, that is to say organized as an identifiable figure (the cone of a mountain), or by definite signs (the fingers of the hand, classical cornices). The two alternatives are illustrated in the work of Richter & Dahl Rocha: on the one hand, buildings such as the New Learning Center on the IMD campus, the New Museum of Contemporary Art in Lausanne, and the Restaurant for Nestlé; on the other hand, apertures that signal the end of the bands or stripes used for the La Prairie Clinic extension, the frames surrounding the housing at "Les Uttins," and the stone walls on both ends of the glazed facades of the Nestlé Headquarters building.

✳

Tact

I would like to pursue one final aspect of the work of Richter & Dahl Rocha, given that it involves a nuance which imbues their architecture with a highly unusual quality. The order, harmony, definition of boundaries, relative timelessness, and willful consistency of form – which together constitute the "signs" of modern beauty – are not enough to distinguish this work from that of other architects who also seek and attain these objectives. We could turn again to Gramsci for a provocative reflection that sheds light on this problem: "It is too easy to be original by doing the opposite of what everyone else is doing; this is just mechanical. It is too easy to speak differently from others, to play with neologisms, whereas it is difficult to distinguish oneself from others without doing acrobatics."[66] Indeed, the work of Richter & Dahl Rocha carefully avoids any type of acrobatics, to the point that it demands considerable attentiveness to be appreciated by the observer. Their buildings actually seem to reject grandiloquence, to defy blunt definitions, to avoid the domain of the "manifesto" occupied by their contemporaries whose works are consumed as "advanced" or (trans)avant-garde products. The technological feat, the formal surprise, the absolute denial, the novel structure: these phenomena are absolutely foreign to Richter & Dahl Rocha's work. They inhabit, we would say, the space of *neutral* production. But we would be mistaken in assuming that there are negative connotations for the attribute of neutrality. Roland Barthes dedicated one of his last lecture courses at the Collège de France (1977–78) to the subject,

---

66 Gramsci, "Sincerity (or Spontaneity) and Discipline," *Selections from Cultural Writings: Problems of Criticism,* ed. David Forgacs and Geoffrey Nowell-Smith, trans. William Boelhower (Cambridge, Mass.: Harvard University Press, 1985), p. 214.

and from his in-depth analysis emerged an illuminating definition: "I call Neutral everything that baffles the paradigm."[67] The "paradigm," for Barthes, is the "motor of meaning," a certain, specific meaning. The paradigm operates within the opposition of clear extremes, among which a conflict is established: it requires the maximum profundity and attainable aspirations. In one or the other direction, the clear meaning upon which the categorical affirmation or negation is founded is thus established. The avant-garde and the moral act upon the paradigm. The Neutral is a state of provoked dysfunction of the paradigm, and therefore leaves us uncertain. Barthes concludes that "the Neutral doesn't refer to 'impressions' of grayness, of 'neutrality', of indifference. The Neutral – my Neutral – can refer to intense, strong, unprecedented states. 'To outplay the paradigm' is an ardent, burning activity…. [The Neutral is] suspended in front of the hardenings of both faith and certitude…. [The subject] finds himself confronted with an aporia: wishing for a logical 'monster', the right mix of emotion and distance…. In short, a well-behaved Eros, 'restrained', 'reserved'."[68]

I have already noted that the work of Richter & Dahl Rocha does not present itself aggressively, but neither is it absolutely silent, in the sense of a total absence of the intent to communicate. Barthes' distinction between the Latin verbs denoting silence is meaningful here. Barthes points to an "interesting nuance" in the difference between the Latin verbs *tacere* (verbal silence) and *silere* ("stillness, absence of movement and of noise").[69] *Tacere* deals with the human domain of the word, verbal expression about the human condition, whereas *silere* connotes the mute serenity typical of objects and natural phenomena ("the night, the sea, the winds"). It would be valid, in that sense, to say that the silence in Richter & Dahl Rocha's work is that of *silere*. But, how do you reconcile *silere* – in the end an extreme, affirmative situation – with that "baffling of the paradigm" that would consist in the option for neutrality, which in my view characterizes their architecture. To describe the state of equilibrium that is opposed to unstable representation, and to avoid transforming silence into a stable element of the paradigm, "the Neutral would be defined not by permanent silence, which, being systematic, dogmatic, would become the signifier of an affirmation ('I am systematically taciturn'), but by the minimal expenditure of a speech act meant to neutralize silence as a sign."[70] I maintain that Richter & Dahl Rocha imbue the work with *silere* in such a manner that it is presented to us in the "state of equilibrium" characteristic of beauty itself, but adjusting or reducing the operation to the maximum possible to the point where silence is neutralized as sign.

Among the many manifestations of the neutral that Barthes explored in his lecture course, I would like to draw particular attention to what he refers to as "the principle of tact."[71] In a universe mandated by the paradigm, the tactful is

67 Roland Barthes, *The Neutral: Lecture Course at the College de France (1977-1978)*, trans. Rosalind E. Krauss and Denis Hollier (New York: Columbia University Press, 2005), p. 6; originally published as *Le Neutre, de Roland Barthes, Notes de cours au Collège de France, 1977–1978, texte établi, annoté et presenté par Thomas Clerc* (Paris: Éditions Du Seuil, 2002).
68 Barthes, *The Neutral*, pp. 7 and 14–16.
69 Ibid., pp. 23f.
70 Ibid., p. 27.
71 Ibid., pp. 29ff.

unimaginable: the culture we construct is expected to be categorical, affirmative, virile. Tactfulness is a feminine principle, therefore weak, secondary, irrelevant. A tactful man is the object of censure, as he occupies a dubious state between man and woman. As Barthes explains it, "the principle of tact is: a pleasure [*jouissance*] in analysis, a verbal operation that frustrates expectation,... a perversion that plays with the useless (nonfunctional) detail."[72] The principle of tact is therefore a kind of politeness, to the extent that it is based in the idea of a pleasurable and voluntary concession to the other. As in the gesture of politeness, the tactful treatment of a work consists in its ability to comprise a certain stroke of need: on the contrary, the paradigmatic manifestation of the discourse beyond the requirements of life that provide meaning to the woks tries to capture the attention of the other. Furthermore, Barthes proposes: "I would suggest calling the nonviolent refusal of reduction, the parrying of generality by inventive, unexpected, nonparadigmatizable behavior, the elegant and discreet flight in the face of dogmatism, in short, the principle of tact, I would call it, all being said: sweetness."[73] In light of Barthes' observations, many courteous gestures in the work of Richter & Dahl Rocha have been revealed in my foregoing remarks, but it is worth calling attention to two other particularly notable cases. One is the way in which in the New Meeting Place on the IMD campus emerges from within the preexisting construction, occupying the exterior space by means of a gentle widening of the floor plan that surrounds – like a protective embrace – the grove of Centennial trees in the park. The other, perhaps more moving example, is the resurrection of the unbuilt cupola Jean Tschumi designed to surmount his double-spiral stairway in the Nestlé Headquarters building. The intent was to illuminate and complete that magnificent example from the history of modern architecture. Given the diameter of the opening over the stairwell, a glazed opening at that scale would have necessitated a cumbersome structure contradicting the architects' intent, in the sense that Barthes construed as the minimal expenditure of a speech act meant to neutralize silence as a sign. Therefore, Richter & Dahl Rocha sought to calibrate their intervention by determining the maximum dimensions of commercial glass available to them, and fabricating a funnel-shaped Fiberglas skylight to mediate the difference between the aperture itself and the glazed oculus, to achieve a presence whose maximum intensity is reached precisely where it is reduced to almost total absence: "to baffle the paradigm" by mediating the hardness of steel to achieve the softest of light.

72 Ibid., p. 29.
73 Ibid., p. 36.

Based on Richter & Dahl Rocha's winning project for the first "Europan" competition on housing (1988–89), the SWHome® concept emerged in response to the building crisis of the 1990s. Richter & Dahl Rocha's aim was to promote a modular, flexible, and easily convertible "do-it-yourself" type of single-family housing, but given social and economic forces, this led to a system applicable to collective living, the SWHome® Housing System. SWHome® explored themes that have predominated recent architectural debates, including the question of how to reconcile the desire for open-plan dwellings that allow inhabitants to express their individual lifestyles with the standardization and industrialization that dominate contemporary construction practices. The development of viable solutions involved going beyond the essential architectural and technical concerns and literally redefining the roles played by inhabitants, architects, engineers, material suppliers, builders, and developers. The architects collaborated with contractors to reflect on key issues and to generate proposals addressing alternative modes of building for new ways of living. SWHome® also instigated reflection

on issues that led to better understanding of how standardized production and commercial distribution can facilitate not just the "bottom line," but optimum housing construction. The notion of "flexibility" was at the forefront of the development of the SWHome® apartment typology. Inside the volume of each apartment, structural elements were carefully positioned, while mechanical systems and conduits of all kinds were integrated into party walls, allowing for partitions and floors to be modified at will. Each unit thus has the capacity to evolve over time as interior spaces are transformed and adapted to the changing needs of inhabitants. The horizontal and vertical network of exterior circulation allows for modular elements to be easily reconfigured, making it possible for diverse architectural and urban patterns to emerge from the deployment of a single construction system, while a wide range of cladding materials express the individual character of each housing unit. Among the few SWHome experiments documented herewhith, the Twin Villas in the Lausanne suburb of Chailly are a peticularly interesting example of how the system can be applied to affortable multi-family housing.

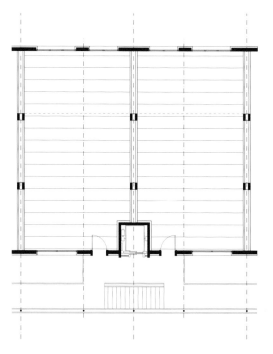
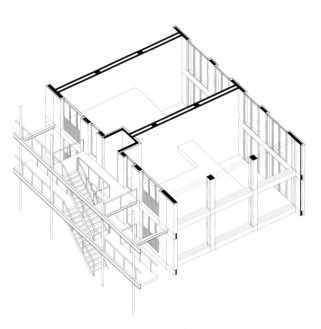

This page: SWHome® Housing System / plan and axonometric view of basic modular unit for two apartments, showing exterior circulation. Opposite, clockwise from top: SWHome® typologies – villa, medium-density apartment building, and high-density urban block.

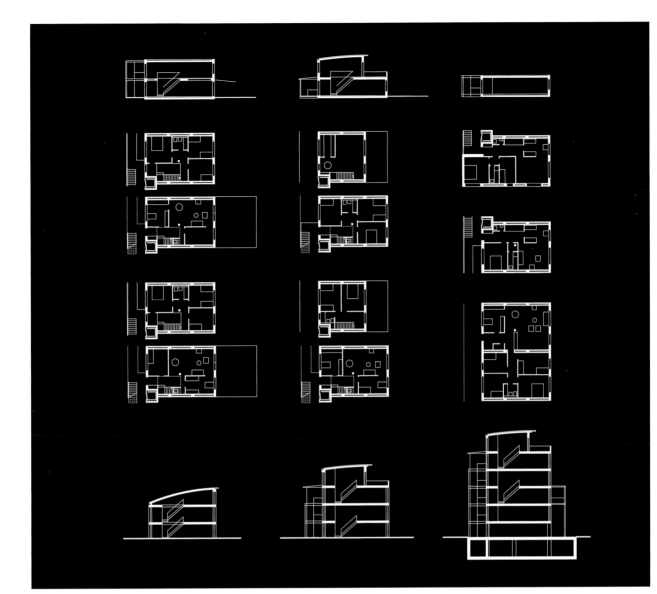

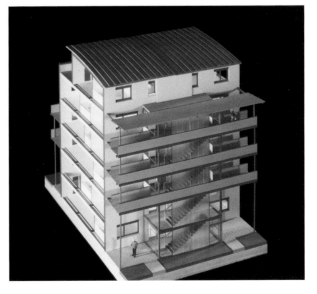

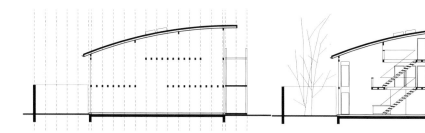

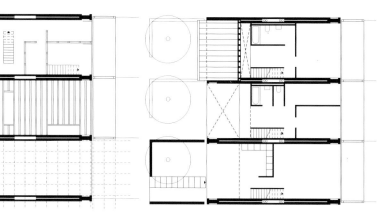

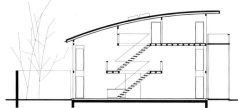

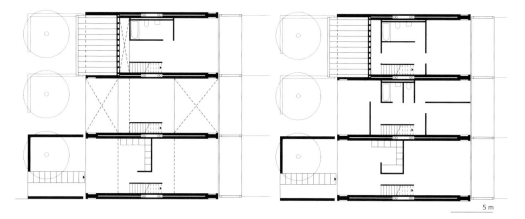

5 m

This page: SWHome® Housing System / plans and sections showing possible configurations of
villa-type units. Opposite: interior and exterior views of the twin villas at Chailly.

PROTOTYPE FOR A FOREST REFUGE
"LA RACINE," GRAND RISOUX FOREST,
CANTON VAUD, SWITZERLAND, 1991–96

Sited in the Grand Risoux Forest in the Jura mountains, the aim of this project was to provide hikers with a place of shelter. A rustic wooden structure of about 25 square meters, the Refuge is simply furnished with a wood-burning stove and a table. The initial brief from the Cantonal Forestry Service proposed the development of a prototype using prefabricated building elements, and thus the design was based on construction elements which could be fabricated in winter and transported to a site for assembly in early spring. Resting lightly on eight concrete piers, the Refuge hovers just above the irregular ground plane of the wooded forest site. The building volume was generated using a series of geometrical transformations applied to the basic typology of the primitive wooden hut. Walls were translated along their axes to free the four angles of the plan, while the ridge of the roof was shifted and aligned diagonally in relation to the quadrilateral plan, creating an irregularly canted roof canopy. Although it was designed according to basic geometric principles, the refuge paradoxically appears to be an "organic" form in tune with the landscape. Unfortunately, the building was destroyed by fire in 2003.

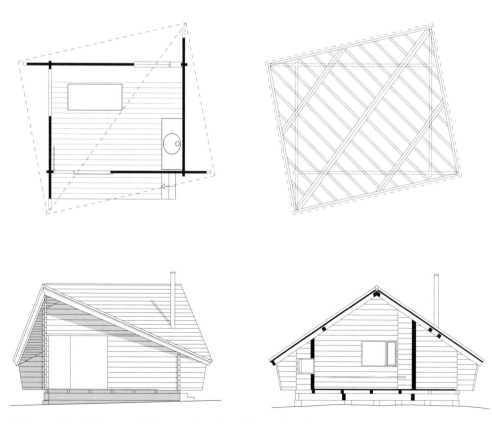

This page, clockwise from upper left: Prototype for a Forest Refuge / plan, roof structure, section, and elevation. Opposite: exterior view of Forest Refuge in summer time.

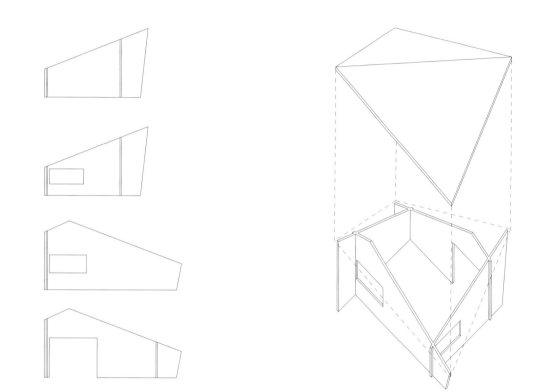

This page, top to bottom: Prototype for a Forest Refuge / diagrams showing how the wall shapes result from their intersection with the pitched roof; views of the assembly process. Opposite: view showing geometry of interior elevation. Following pages: views showing the different geometry of exterior elevations.

Adjacent to the Geneva station, amid a vast network of railroad tracks, this structure of more than 10,000 square meters is dedicated to the maintenance of the new Swiss train configuration. The program includes a service annex to house administrative offices, locker rooms, a kitchen, and other amenities for employees. The Maintenance Center presents itself as a simple volume entirely covered by a series of north-facing sheds with fenestration that brings natural light to the various interior spaces. The irregular plan emerged as the architects sought to maximize the usable space within the constraints of the site, while the architectural idiom was derived from the expression of the materials themselves – primarily the contrast between aluminum and wood – to reinforce the essentially functional character of the building. The main facades, which extend about 300 meters along the railroad tracks, are clad with oversized "shingles" of oil-treated wood, and are protected by deep eaves. For the end-elevations of the long hall as well as for the service annex, a second type of facade, in this case without eaves, was created using aluminum panels.

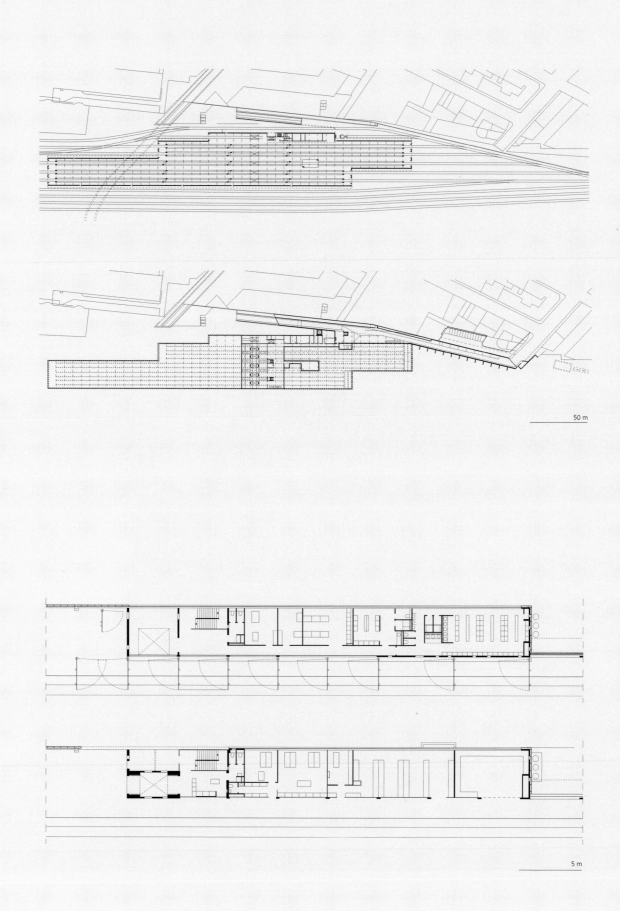

50 m

5 m

This page: Swiss National Train Maintenance Center / view of wood-shingled facade. Opposite, top to bottom: plans of ground-floor, basement, and service annex (first and second floors).

This page: Swiss National Train Maintenance Center / interior views showing
maintenance areas beneath the rails. Opposite: interior view and section.

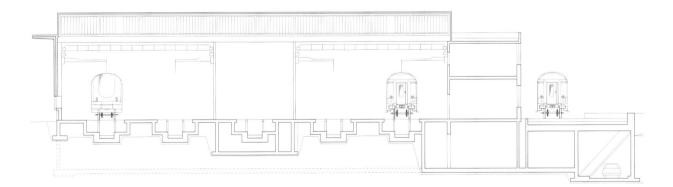

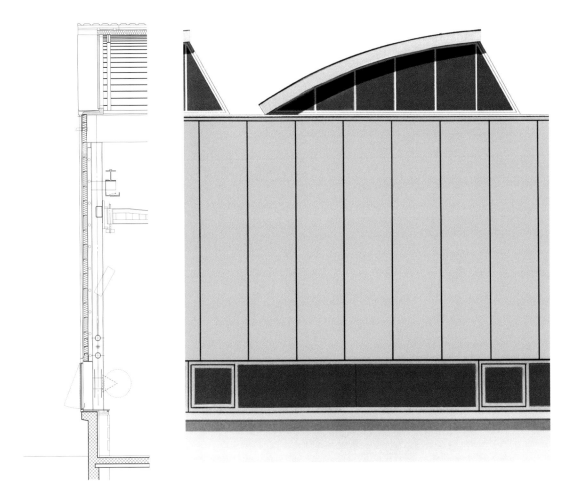

This page: Swiss National Train Maintenance Center / detail in section and elevation of aluminum facade with glazed lateral end of skylight. Opposite: detail in section and elevation of facade with oversized wood shingles, roof overhang, and opaque lateral end of skylight.

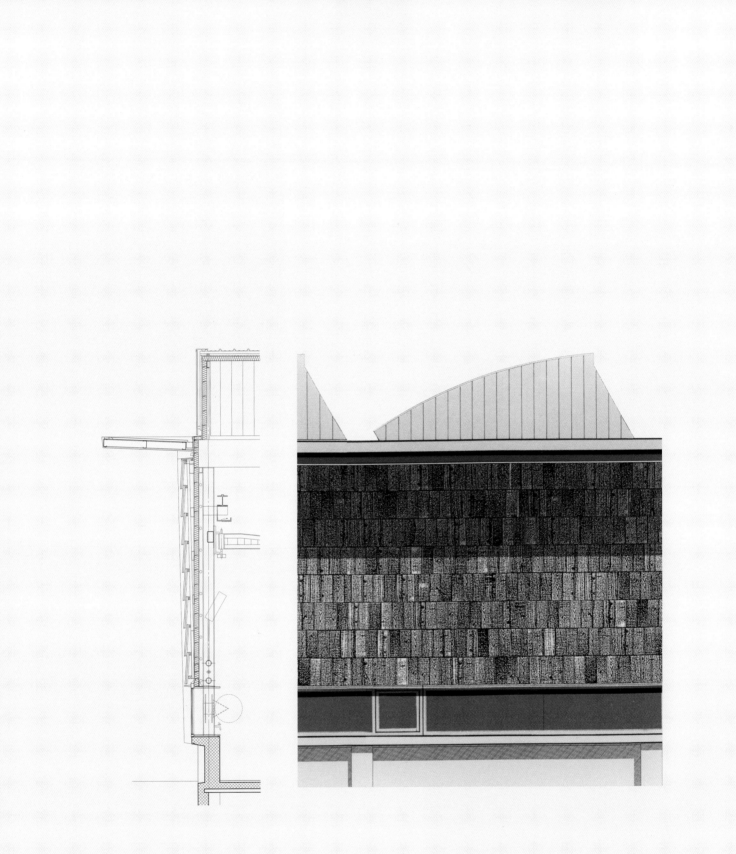

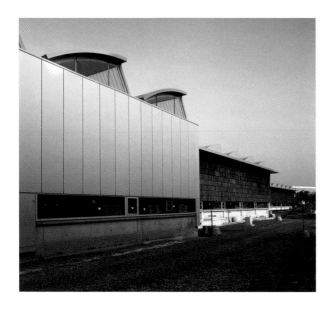

This page and opposite: Swiss National Train Maintenance Center / views showing contrasting wood and aluminum facades.

The Nestlé Headquarters in Vevey is one of the most remarkable examples of postwar modernist architecture in Switzerland. This major work of architect Jean Tschumi was completed in 1960. In 1976, a second, slightly irregular "bar" building was added at the southern end by Martin Burckhardt in partnership with Frédéric Brugger, and the complex was subsequently subjected to a number of transformations and additions. Continuing expanding functional demands, an aging "skin," and the obsolescence of the building's original mechanical systems called for a complete renovation of Tschumi's building, which had in the meantime been designated a historic monument. In 1996, Richter & Dahl Rocha undertook a renovation that effectively implied stripping the building down to its structural elements and reinventing the curtain wall system in light of the most recent technological developments, while guaranteeing a nearly identical appearance and effect. Elements such as the canopied entrances and the double-spiral "Chambord" staircase extending from the first to sixth floors were carefully restored. The magnitude of this operation did not dissuade the architects from making a wider appraisal which resulted in several major interventions: one involving the execution of an element that Tschumi himself had not been able to realize, the Oculus or skylight that now hovers over the Chambord staircase, and others involving completely new elements: The new Liaison Space, a glazed atrium six floors in height comprising stairs and ramps, resolved a problem which had plagued the Burckhardt addition, that is, circulation

between the two buildings. It links Tschumi's building with the bar building at all six levels, richly enhancing the unity and coherence of the whole, even to the point of offering the visitor formerly unavailable prospects of Tschumi's curving lakeside facade. A new suspended staircase leads from the contained executive reception area on the fifth floor to the more public sixth floor, again making a new link between formerly discrete architectural elements. Richter & Dahl Rocha's renovation of a classic modernist building thus posed as many new questions as it sought to respect its landmark status, particularly with respect to the architects' strategic approach and means which involved a complex set of operations at the intersection of restoration and invention, where the conservation and transformation of original aspects of the complex also enabled the creation of new elements.

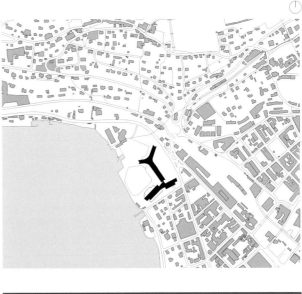

This page and opposite: Nestlé Headquarters / originally designed by Jean Tschumi (1958), with addition by Martin Burckhardt, Burckhardt & Partners (1973–76).

This page: Nestlé Headquarters / Richter & Dahl Rocha's Liaison Space.
Opposite, clockwise from upper left: scheme for ramp distribution, plan of
sixth floor, and section.

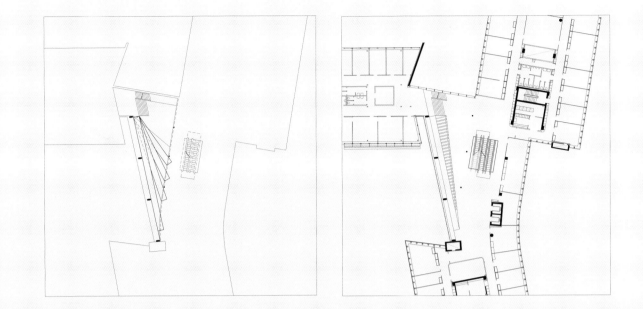

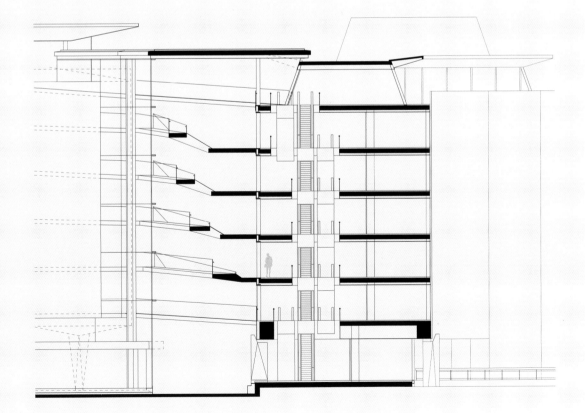

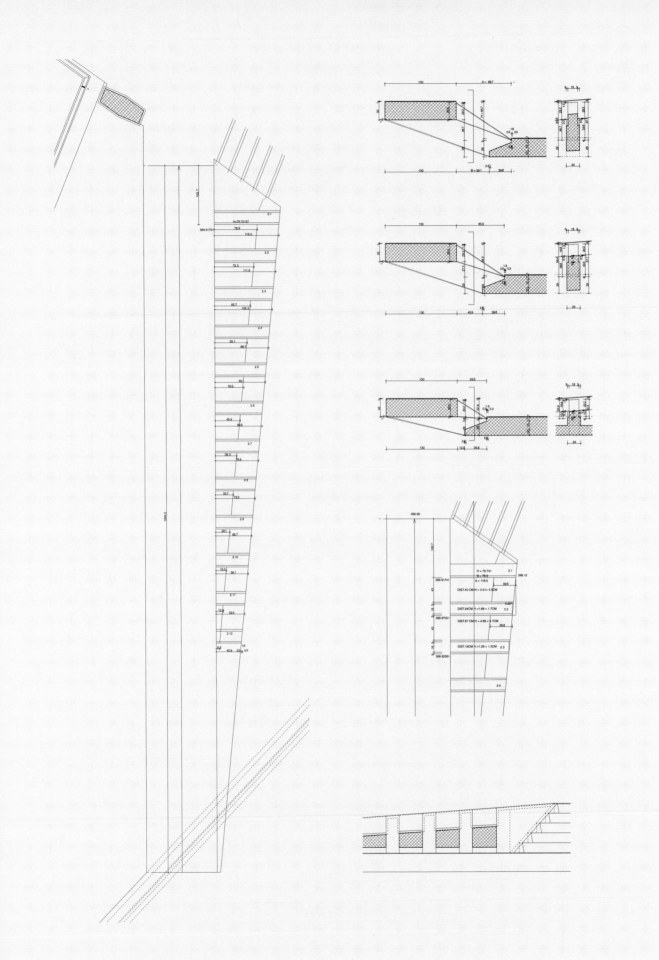

This page: Nestlé Headquarters / Liaison Space, view of circulation ramp.
Opposite: construction detail, ramp.

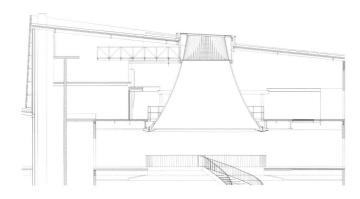

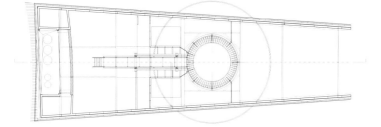

This page, clockwise from upper left: Nestlé Headquarters / construction detail, Oculus, Fiberglas cone of skylight being lifted into position, and Oculus seen from the ground floor looking up through Tchumi's Chambord staircase. Opposite: interior view of Oculus.

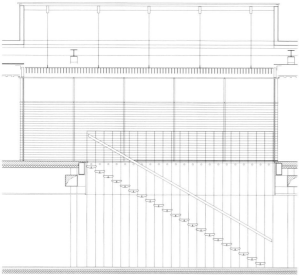

This page: Nestlé Headquarters / view and section of Executive Staircase connecting fifth and sixth floors. Opposite top to bottom: construction detail, Executive Staircase, detail of "suspended" steps, and view of upper landing.

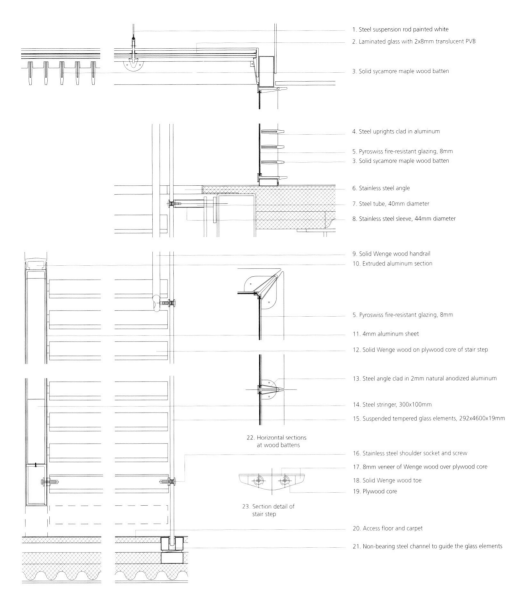

1. Steel suspension rod painted white

2. Laminated glass with 2x8mm translucent PVB

3. Solid sycamore maple wood batten

4. Steel uprights clad in aluminum

5. Pyroswiss fire-resistant glazing, 8mm
3. Solid sycamore maple wood batten

6. Stainless steel angle

7. Steel tube, 40mm diameter

8. Stainless steel sleeve, 44mm diameter

9. Solid Wenge wood handrail
10. Extruded aluminum section

5. Pyroswiss fire-resistant glazing, 8mm

11. 4mm aluminum sheet

12. Solid Wenge wood on plywood core of stair step

13. Steel angle clad in 2mm natural anodized aluminum

14. Steel stringer, 300x100mm

15. Suspended tempered glass elements, 292x4600x19mm

22. Horizontal sections
at wood battens

16. Stainless steel shoulder socket and screw

17. 8mm veneer of Wenge wood over plywood core

18. Solid Wenge wood toe
19. Plywood core

23. Section detail of
stair step

20. Access floor and carpet

21. Non-bearing steel channel to guide the glass elements

The scope of the commission for the renovation of Nestlé Headquarters included not only the architectural elements, but all of the building interiors as well. The reception area was completely redesigned, and custom furniture was created for the executive suite and reception area, the administrative offices, public spaces of the sixth floor, and offices throughout the building. Just inside the main entrance, a reception desk plays against the see-through transparency of the ground floor as a dark line against a glass panel in which the Nestlé logo is etched in a pattern designed by artists Philip Baldwin, Monica Guggisberg, and Paolo Ferro. The reception desk itself, in Wenge wood, hovers mysteriously over a softly reflective base of matte-finished aluminum panels. It appears to "float," supported only by a laminated translucent glass beam. The workspace behind the desk is finished in black leather. For the office spaces, a modular furnishing system was developed in collaboration with dai AG, and produced by Italian manufacturer Unifor Spa. Sycamore maple was used in conjunction with colored fabric and bronze-finished aluminum accents. Components of one basic modular scheme can be combined and adapted to various working configurations. For the new executive suite and reception area as well as administrative offices, the architects designed furnishings, some inspired by Tschumi's original designs of the late 1950s. Again, the play of light and dark was invoked with laminated Wenge wood, in this case in combination with light maple, cream-colored leather, an upholstery fabric made of plant fiber, and anodized aluminum accents.

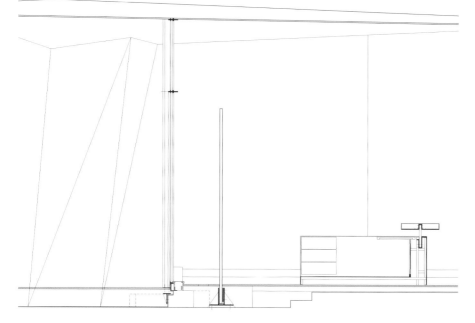

This page and opposite: Nestlé Headquarters / Reception Area, views and section.

This page and opposite: Nestlé Headquarters / Modular Office Furniture System
developed in collaboration with dai AG and produced by Unifor Spa.

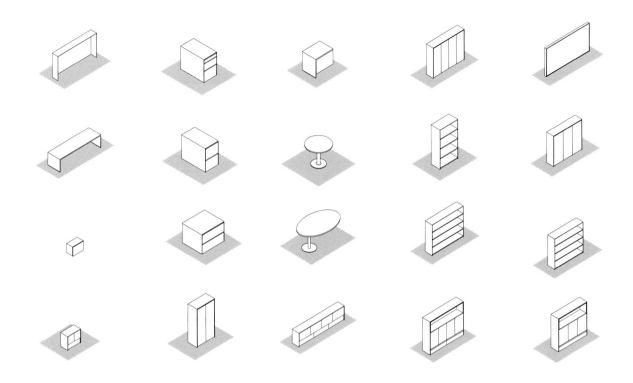

This page and opposite: Nestlé Headquarters / chairs and credenza designed for the Executive Suite and Executive Reception Area. Following pages, top to bottom: desk and conference room furnishings designed for Nestlé's executive director.

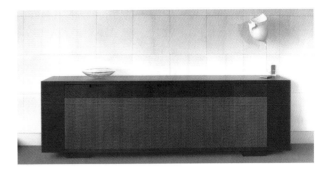

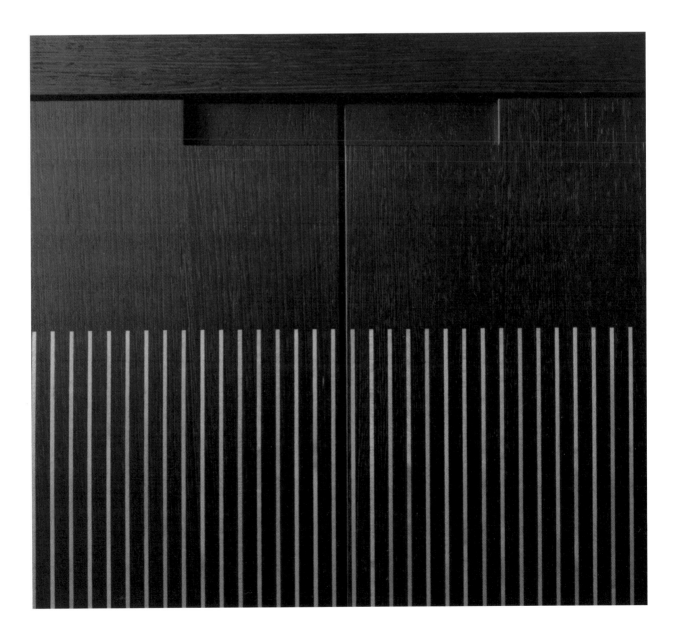

An important consideration in the renovation of the Nestlé
Headquarters was the exploration of the potential of
architecture and graphic design to corporate values and
identity. In addition to evoking a sense of continuity
and timelessness through the key architectural and interior
design moves, the architects realized this potential in the
visual communication strategies they employed to carry
the Nestlé logo. The famous "bird's nest" is not only etched
in the large glass screen of the reception area, but is also
woven into the stage curtain for the Meeting Hall on the
sixth floor, translated into an aluminum and inlaid in Wenge
wood for a podium in a meeting room, and displayed as a
marble cutout against dark Plexiglas on the building facade,
where it is backlit at night to be seen from the road.

This page: Nestlé Headquarters / assembly and installation of company logo on building facade. Opposite, clockwise from upper left: various versions of the logo in aluminum and wood (meeting room, speakers platform), woven fabric (Meeting Hall projection screen), and etched glass (Reception Area).

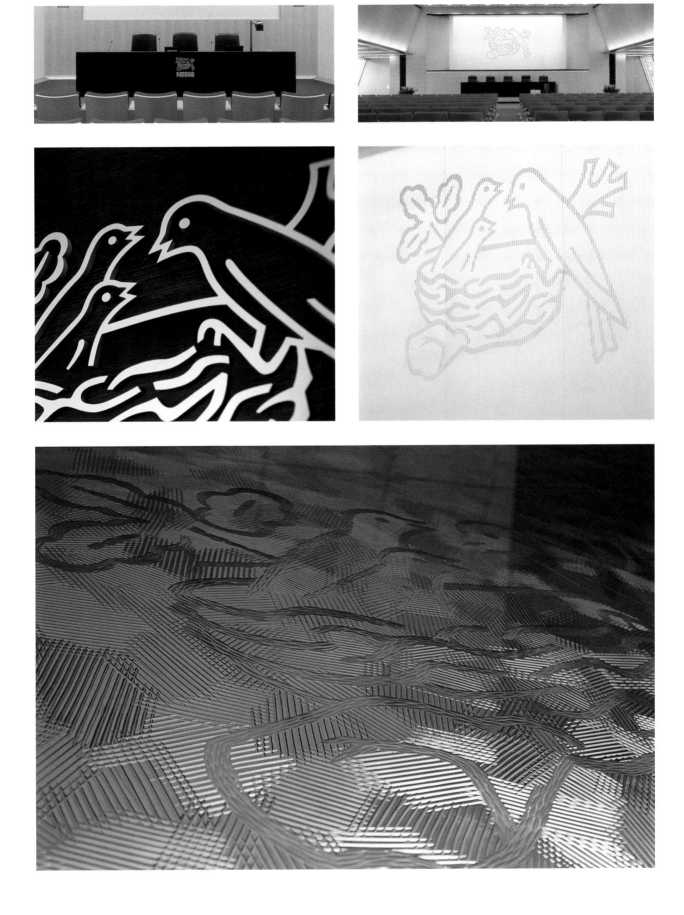

The firm occupies part of an old masonry house located in a residential neighborhood of five- to six-story apartment buildings. Three different elements were combined to create this office complex of 1,350 square meters: the first floor of the house, which faces the street; an abandoned warehouse located directly behind the house; and the back and side of another building located in the same block. Behind the formal facade of the old building, the irregular plan "invades" the regularity of the typical housing typology of this neighborhood, infusing the residual space situated at the heart of a housing block with a new dynamic. A major thrust of the intervention was the creation of an independent entrance for the office; likewise, there was a strong focus on articulating the circulation between the abandoned warehouse space and the residential structure. The new entrance leads to a monumental staircase, which as it ascends two stories is traversed by a "bridge" constructed of raw steel members suspended from the stairwell ceiling. Enclosed with etched glass and steel mesh, this bridge which connects the two parts of

the studio reveals the blurry silhouettes of figures passing from one side to the other. Open spaces for design staff to work in teams are deployed on two levels – the original floor of the warehouse and a newly created mezzanine – while offices and conference rooms are located in the masonry house. Plywood furniture was designed to create a warm and inviting atmosphere throughout, while the raw industrial character of the warehouse was preserved through the use of exposed steel beams, large industrial windows and doors, and roughly finished floors.

This page, clockwise from upper left: Richter & Dahl Rocha Office / view from Parc de Milan, sideview of entrance portico, and plan of ground floor and mezzanine. Opposite: view into glazed foyer of main entrance.

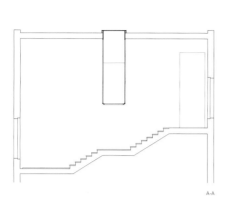

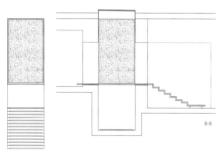

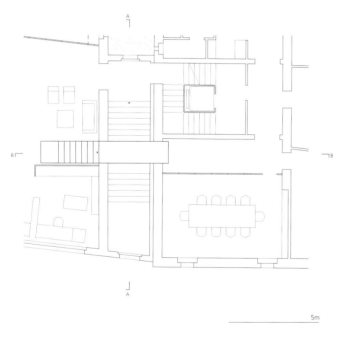

5m

This page, top to bottom, left and right: Richter & Dahl Rocha Office / section drawings and plan showing "bridge" element suspended above monumental entrance staircase, and views revealing light and shadow effects as bridge element crosses the staircase. Opposite: "folded" steel staircase leading up to bridge element from the main floor.

CUSTOM FURNITURE DESIGNS FOR
HUGHES CHEVALIER, INC. (PARIS)
LAUSANNE / PARIS / MILAN 1998–2000

Collaboration with the Paris-based furniture manufacturer
Hughes Chevalier started shortly after the completion of
the Nestlé Headquarters renovation. A few furniture
pieces, initially designed for Nestlé, were revised for
production and marketing by the French firm, and these
were augmented by new pieces designed to form a living
room ensemble. An ongoing collaboration with Hughes
Chevalier, this project also included the design, prodution,
and marketing of a chair and stool. RDR design SA, a
division of Richter & Dahl Rocha Architects, is currently
working on a light restaurant chair, as well as a dining
room ensemble. These furniture designs are executed
primarily with light and dark wood laminations combined
with colored leather upholstery.

VILLA LA FALAISE /
RENOVATION & EXPANSION FOR THE UNION OF
EUROPEAN FOOTBALL ASSOCIATIONS (UEFA)
NYON, SWITZERLAND, 1999–2000

An early 20th-century villa located on the banks of Lake
Geneva was entirely renovated to accommodate the
administrative activities of the UEFA. Situated in close
proximity to the organization's main headquarters designed
by architect Patrick Berger, the villa was transformed and
extended to meet the requirements of a program that
includes offices on the second floor, two conference rooms
at ground level, and an open-plan work space at the lower
ground level. Although the entrance facade was restored
to its original state, the contemporary architectural language
of the intervention was expressed on the considerably
modified south elevation. The perimeter of the lower
ground floor was enlarged to increase the available work
space, and natural light was brought in at this level through
lateral patios as well as a new staircase connecting the
lower ground and ground floors. This glass-enclosed staircase volume opening onto an expansive wooden deck is
screened off with louver-like horizontal glass panes to
preserve the openness of the facade and the view toward
the lake.

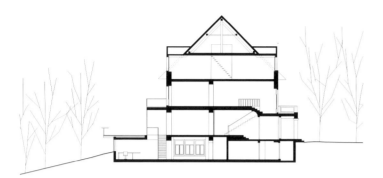

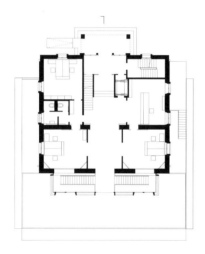

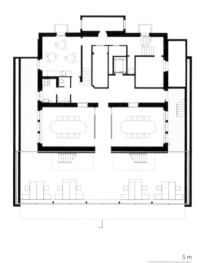

5 m

This page, top to bottom: Villa La Falaise / section and plans of ground and lower ground floors.
Opposite: view showing the addition at lower ground level, lit from above by the double-height
space enclosing the staircase.

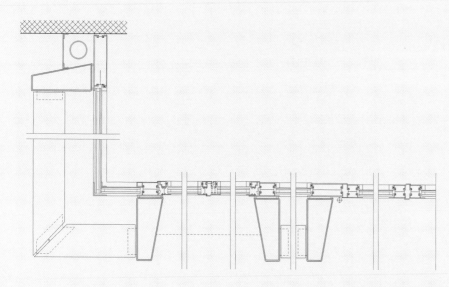

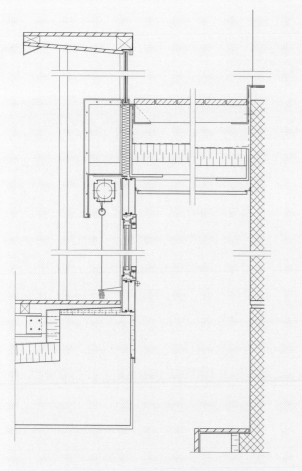

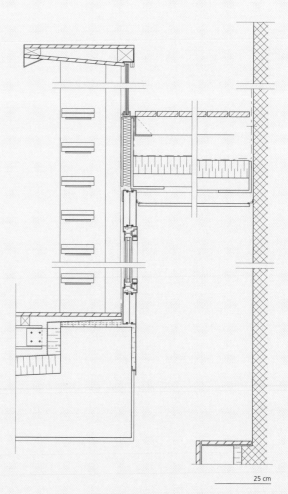

25 cm

This page, top and bottom: Villa La Falaise / views showing glass-louvered facade. Opposite: construction details in plan and section, glass bays with traditional roll-up solar protection and horizontal glass louvers.

This project involved the extension of a school designed
by architects Max Richter & Marcel Gut in the 1960s,
located in a quiet residential neighborhood in the
northwestern sector of Lausanne. The new extension,
a long, narrow bar building, houses a gymnasium at the
lower levels, four new classrooms, and a nursery school
on the upper floor. It follows the northern perimeter
of the site, and thus preserves most of the land for outdoor
games and activities. The base of the building is treated
in concrete and anchored to the sloping terrain, while
the upper floor presents itself as a light wooden pavilion.
To mediate its imposing dimensions, the gymnasium
is half buried in the ground, a strategy that also allows for
natural lighting of the interior spaces while at the same
time creating a "roof terrace" that enlarges the outdoor
space devoted to playgrounds.

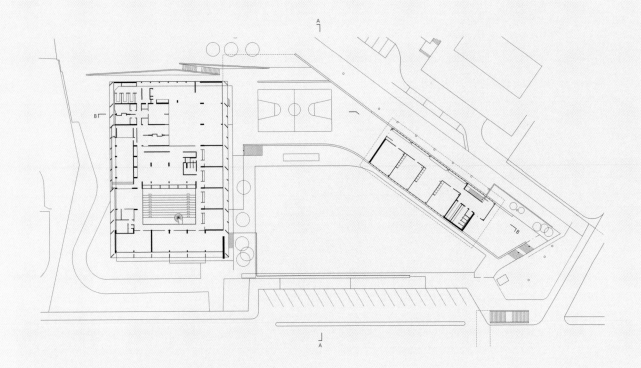

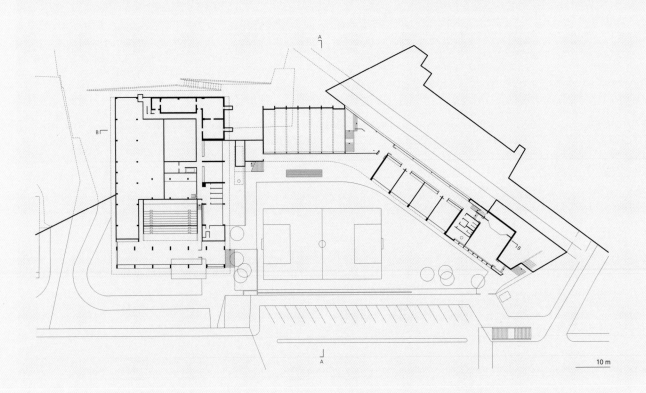

10 m

This page: Valmont Boarding School / schoolyard and playground.
Opposite, top to bottom: plans of ground and first floors.

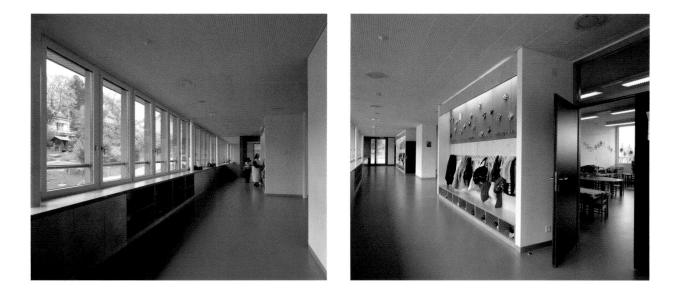

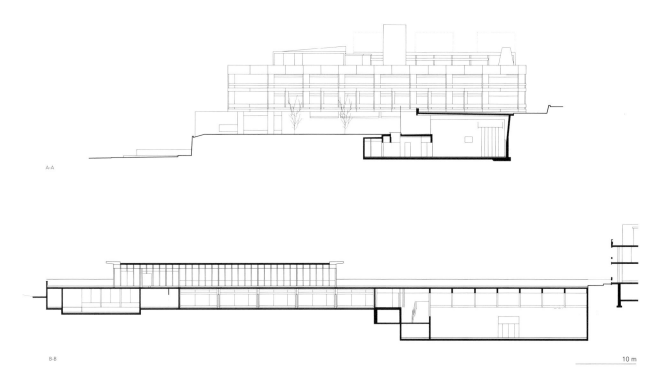

A-A

B-B

10 m

This page, top to bottom: Valmont Boarding School / interior views of hallway and classrooms, section through gymnasium, and longitudinal building section. Opposite: skylit corridor leading to gymnasium. Following pages, double spread: view through glazed facade to double-height gymnasium interior.

This project consists of a series of buildings, essentially a new neighborhood in its own right, near the old center of the medieval town of Rolle on the shore of Lake Geneva between the two major urban centers Geneva and Lausanne. Just walking distance from both the center of the town and the lake, "Les Uttins" consists of three commercial and administrative buildings (A, B, and C) and four apartment buildings (D, E, F, and G). Presented here is the first apartment complex, "The Oaks" (D). This building houses 28 units with the uncommon feature of dual orientation to their lush park setting and the nearby lake. Its shape is the result of combining a series of long horizontal planes forming terraces and balconies facing the park with three compact volumes containing the apartments. It thus appears to have a dual nature: From the road, the volumes of the three housing blocks stand out and suggest a medium-scale housing typology, while from the park, the project presents itself as a more unified whole (the continuity of the terraces evokes the bar building typology) that merges with the landscape. This composition is overlaid on a lower ground floor that contains the access halls for each apartment block, as well as corresponding parking spaces and cellars. This level extends beneath each block like a continuous foundation plate, interrupted only by two little patios inserted between the volumes, allowing for natural light to illuminate the entrance halls and parking spaces. The two entrances to the complex are located at this lower level, one at each end of the building. The lateral positioning of the entrances permitted the creation of private gardens for all apartments at ground level.

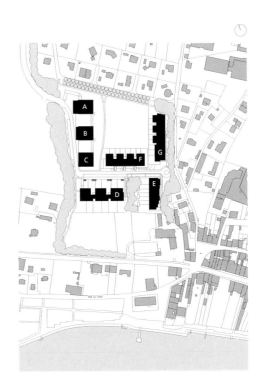

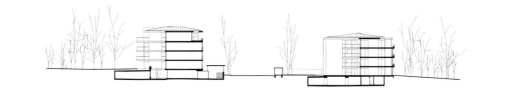

10 m

This page, top to bottom: Residential Development "Les Uttins" / aerial view, section
through buildings F and D, and section through building E. Opposite: view of main
street with building D to the left, and F to the right.

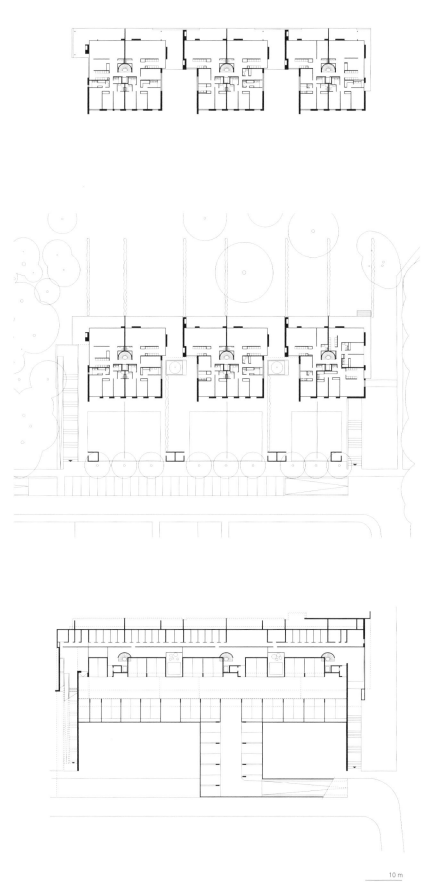

10 m

This page, top to bottom: Residential Development "Les Uttins" / plans of first, ground, and lower ground floors of building D, "The Oaks." The lateral entrance porticos lead to a long entrance hall naturally lit by three exterior patios, providing access to the three housing blocks via circular staircases and elevators. Opposite: view of building D.

This page, top to bottom: Residential Development "Les Uttins" / views showing fragmentation of building D into three blocks, facade composition, and entrance portico. Opposite: northwest entrance, building D.

This page: Residential Development "Les Uttins" / views showing terraces on three levels. Opposite: oculus above the circular staircases and view of entrance hall. Previous pages, double spread: view showing south elevation of building D, facing the lake, where long balconies unify all three blocks creating the effect of a "bar" building.

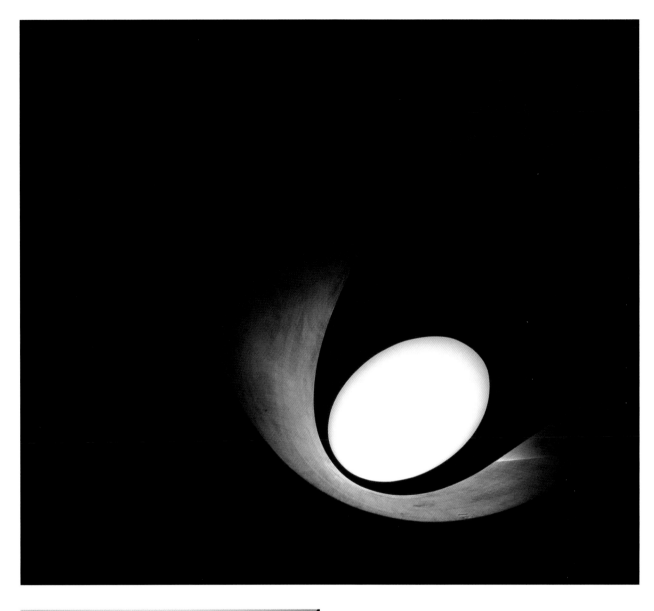

The building for the New Learning Center is located at
the heart of a growing campus, and strategically articulates
between the existing part of the IMD complex to the east
and a future extension to the west, poised between the
more traditional aspects of the institution and new modes
of teaching and learning involving innovative technologies.
As IMD students move through a variety of spaces ranging
from large auditoriums to smaller rooms dedicated to
group work and discussion (and equipped with the latest
technological amenities), they are intended to experience
learning as a creative process. Another major architectural
concern was to subtly integrate the mass of the building
with this relatively small and complex site. The three
upper levels of the building were elevated above ground
level on the sloping hillside site and suspended over the
lobby area at ground level. Thus the building appears
to "float" above the park, facilitating circulation beneath
and through it and preserving the views toward the
surroundings and Lake Geneva. The "skin" of the builing
was conceived with a related intent, that is, to reflect the
sky and the foliage of the trees, and to create the effect of
transparency while bringing natural light to interior
learning spaces.

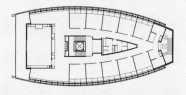

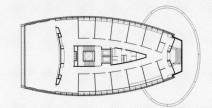

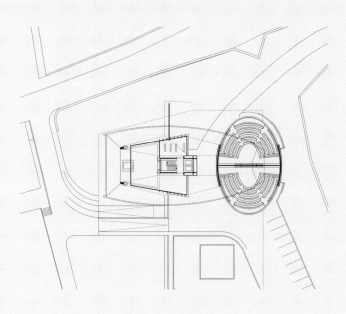

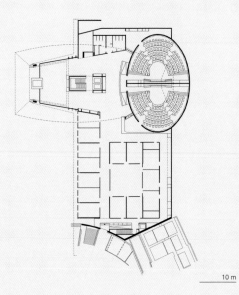

10 m

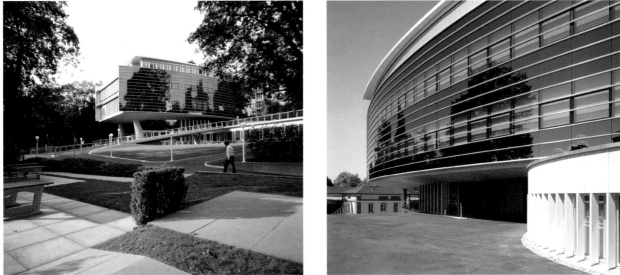

This page: New Learning Center, IMD / exterior views. Opposite page, top to bottom: plans of attic, typical floor, ground floor, and lower ground floor.

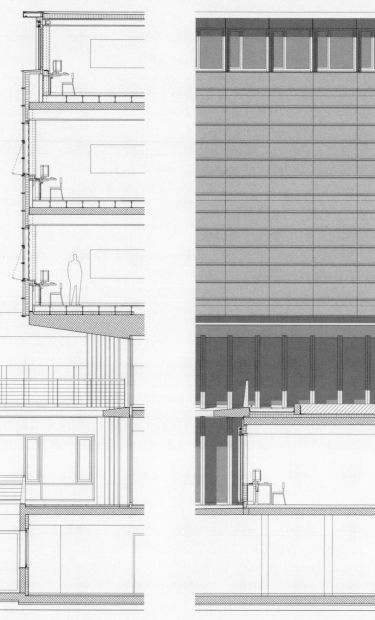

2m

This page: New Learning Center, IMD / view of east facade. Opposite: construction detail in section and elevation, facade.

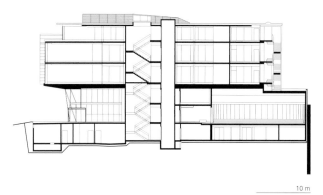

This page, top to bottom: New Learning Center, IMD / longitudinal section and interior views. Opposite: entrance hall.

VILLA SAGER
JEDDAH, SAUDI ARABIA, 1999–2007

This private villa is located in a residential neighborhood in the northern sector of Jeddah. Following a strategy typical of houses in this region, a high perimeter wall encloses the site. Inside this wall, the house itself is composed of two L-shaped volumes that form the two main facades and define several outdoor spaces of different character. At ground level, the house is divided into two distinct zones, one for women and the other for men, with their separate entrances and reception areas. Also at ground level are the kitchen, and a dining room, and an outdoor kitchen. Private family quarters, including bedrooms and baths, occupy the

entire upper floor. The various spaces of the house all converge around a central courtyard which is partially enclosed by glass and partly open to the sky. This courtyard is sheltered by a series of large wooden beams that support the roof while acting as a brise-soleil. The house has massive walls of concrete and stone, with windows, doors, and vertical brise-soleil elements executed in darkly bronzed anodized aluminum and wood.

10 m

This page: Villa Sager / plans of first and ground floors.
Opposite, top to bottom: entrance for women, and entrance for men.

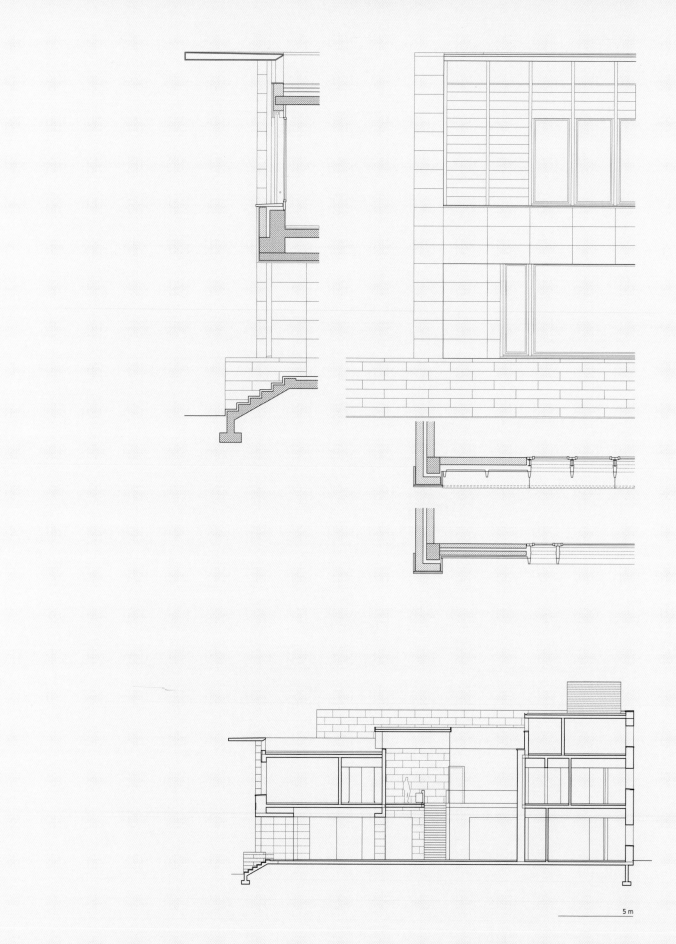

5 m

This page: Villa Sager / sketch of courtyard. Opposite, clockwise from upper left: construction detail, facade, and section through courtyard.

Architecture and graphic design are likewise integrated seamlessly in the facade of the new Nestlé retail store. This storefront facade was approached as a large "billboard" that dynamically represents three different versions of the corporate logo imprinted on vertical louvers of aluminum and glass to produce an optical effect: Each individual louver carries three fragments, which when assembled side by side recreate the complete logo images. The effect of

movement and the superposition of images is activated as the visitor walks from the parking lot toward the entrance alongside the facade.

This page: Nestlé Headquarters / view of Company Store facade showing how three different versions of the Nestlé logo shift to produce the optical illusion. Opposite: construction details in plan and section showing how the logo image is broken down and recomposed for this application.

PROTOTYPE

47,7 cm

5,3 cm

144.6 cm

ELEVATION

SECTION

LEFT-HAND SIDE OF VERTICAL GLASS PANES

RIGHT HAND-SIDE OF VERTICAL GLASS PANES

144.6 cm

PLAN

LEFT-HAND SIDE

RIGHT-HAND SIDE

5,3 cm   2 cm   12,66 cm

The building at Singen belongs to a group of product technology centers (PTC) designed by Richter & Dahl Rocha for Nestlé. Unlike other Nestlé PTC projects undertaken by the firm, all of which were interventions or extensions involving existing buildings, the project at Singen called for the conception of an entirely new structure. The program for the project is distributed over three floors: a large "pilot" plant, development kitchens, and public product testing areas on the ground floor, laboratories and a cafeteria on the first floor, and offices on the upper floor. Due to specific requirements pertaining to floor height and climate control for the pilot plant, floor levels vary between the front part of the building which houses offices and labs and develops on three levels, and the rear part of the plant which comprises two levels: the working area at ground level and a "walk-on" ceiling above. The juxtaposition of these two different typologies led to the L-shaped cross-section of the building, which is noticeable from the outside causing the building to appear to be a simple extrusion of the L-shaped geometry

of the section. The lateral facades are treated as "slices" through the extruded volume by means of the architect's choice of translucent polycarbonate paneling. For the long facades, a beige-colored brick was used to better integrate the building to its surroundings – an industrial site characterized by the presence of late 19th- and early 20th-century buildings displaying similar beige brick facades. However, unlike the older structures, the thin brick panels for the Singen PTC were suspended on light steel frames in accordance with contemporary building technology. The horizontal composition of the brick facades juxtaposed with the treatment of the side elevations reinforces the sense of extension that the composition evokes. On the east facade, a highly visible over-scale Nestlé logo was imprinted on the translucent paneling, signifying the company's presence at the site.

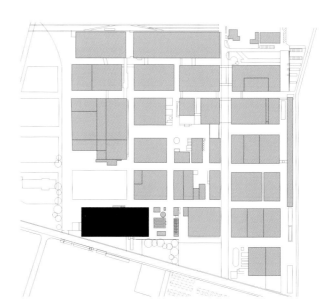

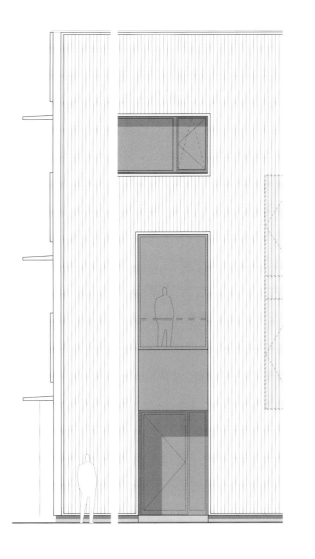

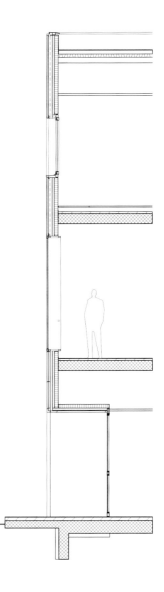

This page, top to bottom: Nestlé Product Technology Center / construction details in elevation and section, polycarbonate facade, views showing junction of two different facade compositions. Opposite, top to bottom: construction detail in elevation and section, brick-clad facade and exterior view.

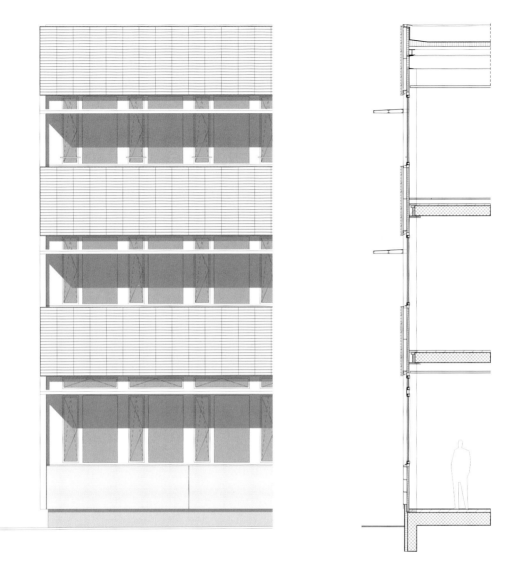

2 m

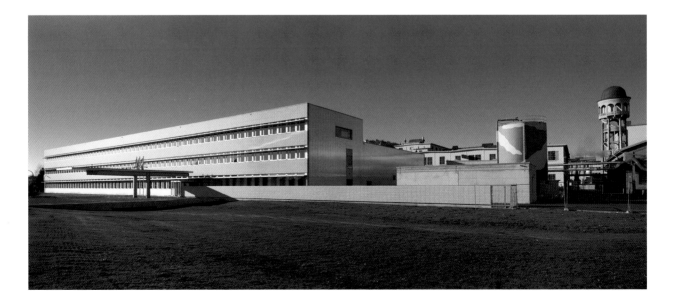

This page, clockwise from upper left: Nestlé Product Technology Center / detail of polycarbonate facade, interior view of production plant, and general view. Opposite, top to bottom: plans of first and ground floors, and section.

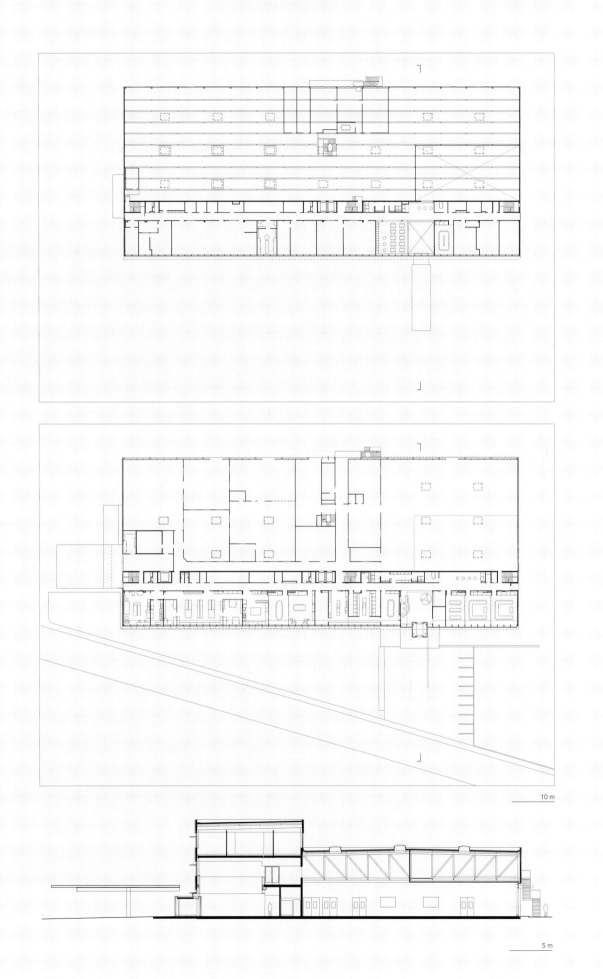

10 m

5 m

This project was developed for a competition launched by the city of Lausanne for the design of a new city hall in the heart of the city, at the northwest end of Lausanne's former industrial core known as "Le Flon." In recent years, like many such quarters in major cities around the world that were abandoned following the decline of local industrial production, this zone is now gradually being recuperated. As new life has been breathed into the area, it has become a focal point of urban activity. Le Flon now offers ideal locations for the mixed-use development of live-work spaces, offices, studios, galleries, theaters, shops, and restaurants. Another unique aspect of Le Flon is its topography. Through this relatively flat area lying at the bottom of a valley just below the level of the historic center of the city, a (now underground) river once flowed. As the site level shifts in relation to its surroundings, a series of bridges cross it, connecting the two upper elevations of the valley. Richter & Dahl Rocha's program includes administrative offices for the city, as well as office and commercial spaces that would be leased to private tenants. Their project is

broken into five buildings which recreates the volumes of demolished warehouses that once occupied the site. At the same time, it creates urban spaces for public gatherings as well as passageways and paths allowing pedestrians access to the neighborhood. To account for the change of level between the ground and upper levels of the city to the north, part of the complex functions as a passerelle in conjunction with a public elevator. In their architectural expression, the five structures plays with the opposition between open and opaque facades, a move that orients each one individually within the larger compass of the site.

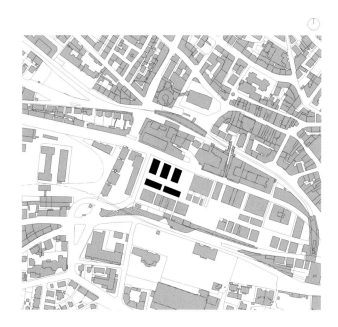

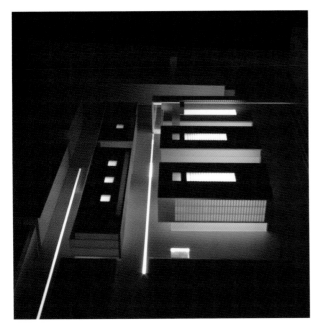

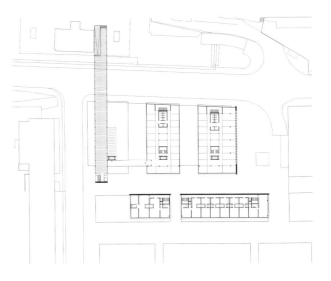

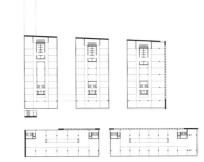

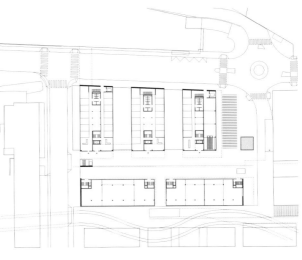

This page, top to bottom: "Flon-Ville" City Hall / plans of upper floor showing *passerelle*, typical floor, and ground floor. Opposite: three sections showing the volumetric fragmentation of the project, and presentation model.

25 m

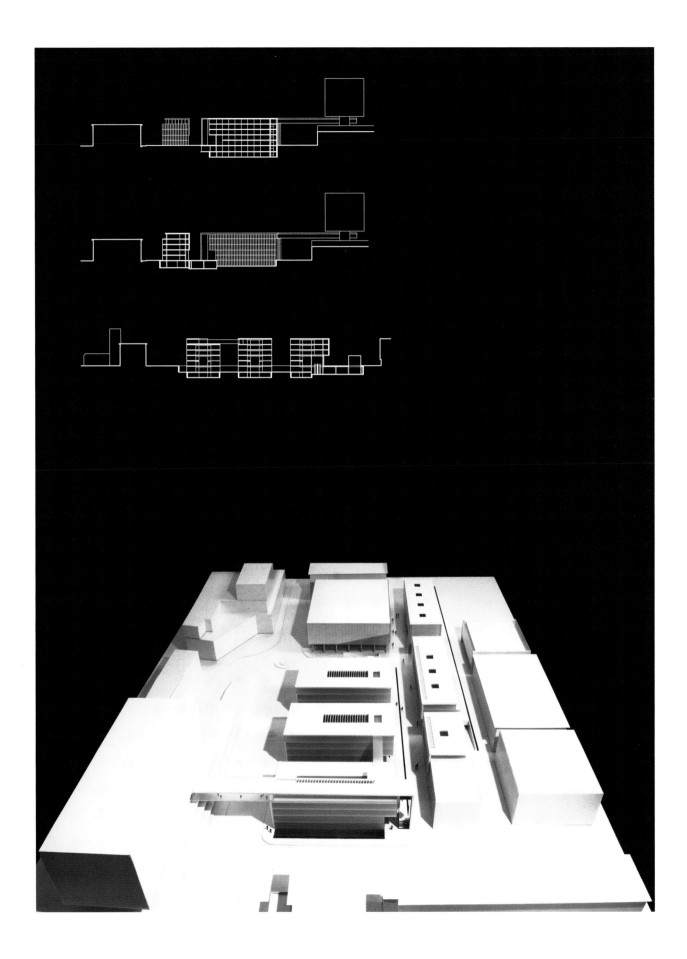

This building is located at the outskirts of Lausanne, along one of the main north-south access roads. The simple volume results in part from a rather straightforward programmatic demand, the commercial leasing of office spaces, but was also informed by municipal regulations that defined the outline of the building and the construction of an attic story. At ground level, the building volume rests on pilotis that allow circulation through access porticos. Though the building presents itself from three sides as a concrete monolith treated in exposed concrete, a white cement with aggregates derived from a yellow stone found in the Jura mountains, the facade toward the road is radically different. This entire elevation is composed of a glazed skin sheltered by a series of aluminum and glass vertical louver elements or brise-soleil. These differ from similar wing-shaped elements in that only two-thirds of the area of each louver is opaque; the remaining third is a tined glass. Even when completely closed, the louvers still allow natural light to pass into the building, and conversely, connect the interior spaces with the surrounding context. As these are controlled independently by the occupants of the various interior spaces, the position of each varies, creating a pattern of movement on the facade. The alternation of aluminum and glass and the resulting play of light and shadow also contribute to the animation of this elevation of the building.

This page: Office Building at Route de Berne 46 / aerial view. Opposite page, top to bottom: plans of attic floor, typical floor, and ground floor. Following pages, clockwise from upper left: entrance portico, main lobby, and view showing how the appearance of the facade varies as occupants adjust the louvered elements to their needs.

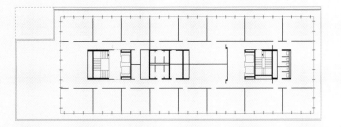

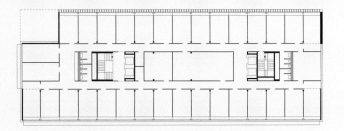

10 m

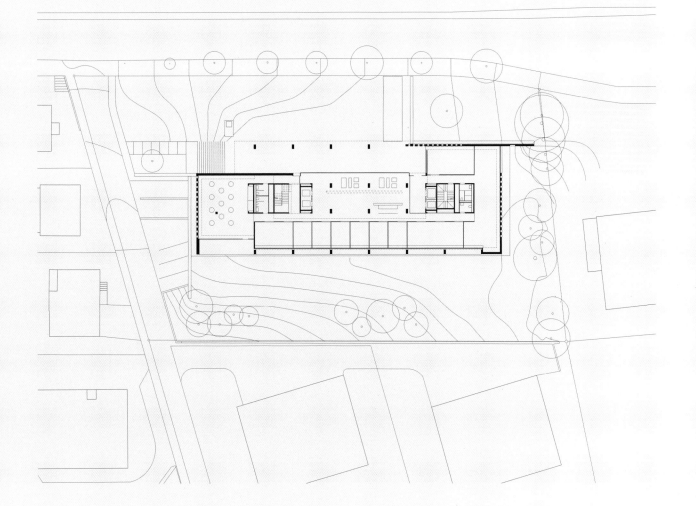

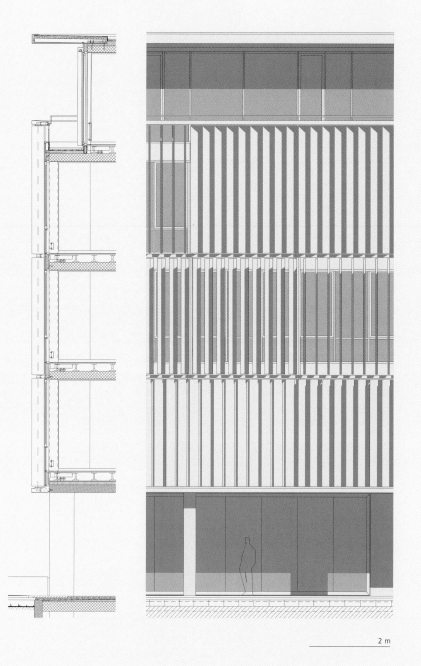

2 m

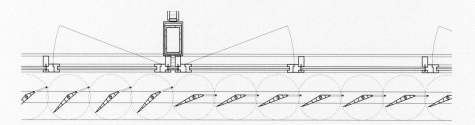

This page: Office Building at Route de Berne 46 / detail of louvered facade.
Opposite page: construction detail in plan, section and elevation, louvered facade.

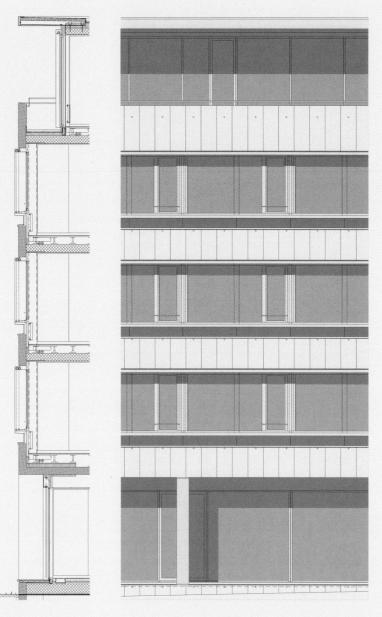

2 m

This page: Office Building at Route de Berne 46 / view of concrete facade.
Opposite page: construction detail in section and elevation, concrete facade.

Situated in Clarens, overlooking Lake Geneva, this clinic founded by the eminent surgeon Paul Niehans has been operating since the 1930s. Before the extension project, La Prairie Clinic occupied two buildings: the "Residence," where the original clinic was born, and a more recent glass and steel building housing modern medical facilities. In addition to these, the Clinic then acquired a larger piece of land and another building, the "Château." The new extension is constructed as a set of walled terraces blending into the Clinic's park, at the intersection of all three other existing edifices. A sinuous stonewall was created using small horizontal pieces of a green stone found in Andeer, in the Canton Grisons, recuperated remainders from the production of a stone quarry laid using a mortar-free technique. The program – a reception area and bar, two pools with complete spa and fitness facilities, and a restaurant – unfolds into spaces that occupy the interval between the new wall and the existing retaining wall of the "Château." The choice of such a subtle intervention was motivated by the architects' desire to preserve and reinforce the natural character of a site understood rather in terms of a rich pre-existing landscape – that of the local vineyards – than as a neutral plot to be built on. The building's spatial structure extends and reaches out to the other existing buildings via spacious passages, allowing for a more comfortable and unified circulation within the complex. Though the building's three levels are semi-buried into the ground, a central theme of the project remains that of natural lighting. Light is modulated as it goes through the thick stonewall and the green roofing of each terrace. For example, a series of skylights were built on top of the swimming pool area as well as through the inner surface of the pool itself, allowing daylight to filter through water and reach the inner corridor of the floor below.

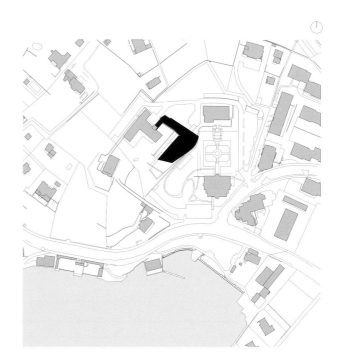

This page: La Prairie Clinic / exterior views. Opposite page, top to bottom: aerial view showing main elevation, and section through swimming pool. Following pages, double spread: general view showing integration of the extension into the terraced site.

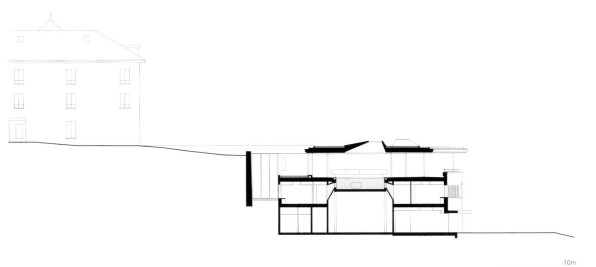

153

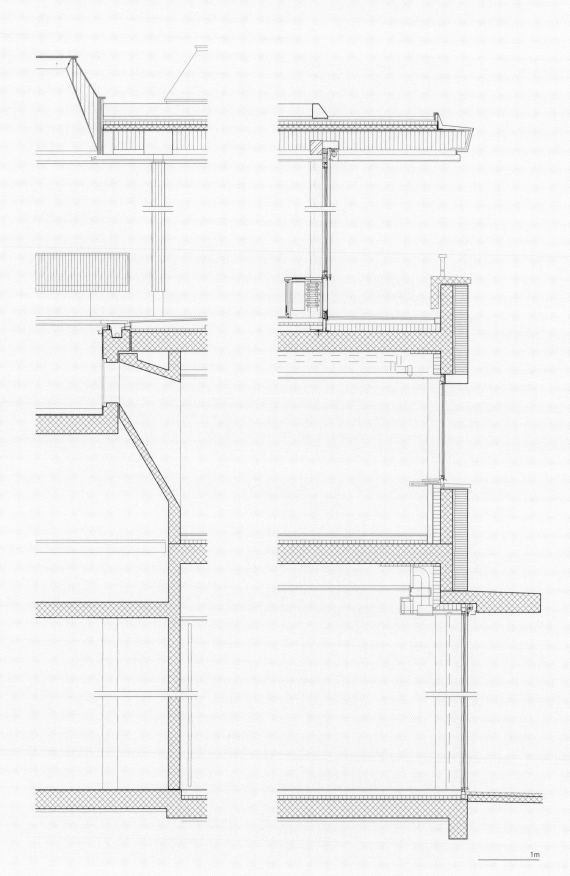

1m

This page: La Prairie Clinic / detail of south elevation. Opposite page: sections showing how light travels from the skylight above the pool area through the lateral wall of the pool into the circulation corridors below.

This page and opposite: La Prairie Clinic / detail and general view of skylights on roof terrace.

This page, top to bottom: La Prairie Clinic / interior views of reception area, lobby, and circulation.
Opposite page, top to bottom: plans of ground-level floor (with reception area, lobby, and pool), first lower-level floor (with treatment rooms), and second lower-level floor (with terrace, restaurant, and kitchens).

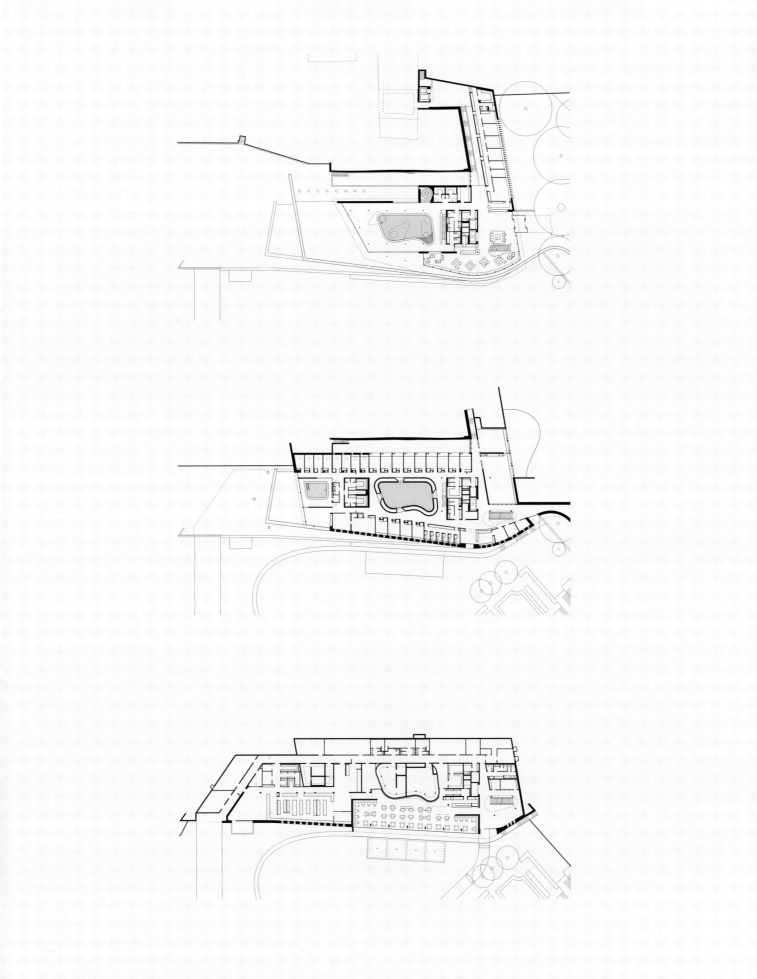

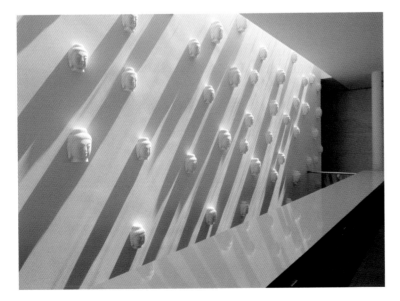

This double page and following pages: La Prairie Clinic / views showing pool area with art installation by Daniel Schlaepfer, first lower-level floor with reception desk for treatement area, circulations corridors and free-form windows looking into the pool.

Located on the banks of Lake Geneva, the city of Montreux benefits from a particularly gentle climate giving it a Mediterranean character. It has become, since the 19th century, a popular tourism and pilgrimage destination, especially for affluent international visitors. The city is well known for its elegant hotels and residences facing the Lake. The project called "La Verrière" consists of the renovation of a long and narrow existing building distinctive mainly for the glasshouse – an old winter garden located at its west end – that was integrated to the renovated part of the project. Inserted between this ancient masonry building, just behind the famous Montreux Palace, and the train tracks leading to the Montreux station, two tall residential buildings were erected, with their back leaning on the railway and their main facade completely open towards the lake. For these new constructions – two glass and brick volumes inserted into the sloping terrain and supported, at street level, by a series of concrete pilotis – the main architectural challenge was to break with the traditional apartment typology of single-level dwelling

units in order to provide floor heights appropriate to the proportions of living spaces. To do so, each apartment is deployed on two different levels. Facing the lake, are living rooms with dramatic ceiling heights, while rooms surrounding the interior courtyard – bedrooms, baths, kitchens, and dining rooms – have avarage ceiling heights. A series of two different typologies perceptible mainly through the project's section thus overlap, both vertically and horizontally. In order to rationalize construction and articulate the "L" shape plan of each flat into a compact volume, all flats were distributed around a generous inner courtyard, the sides of which are composed of glass bricks to allow maximum income of light into the circulations and creating interesting shadows as the inhabitants move around their respective homes. The facade facing the lake, all in glass, is protected by a series of horizontal shades located at the edge of the balconies, blurring the distinction between inside and outside and conveying a sense of lightness to the whole.

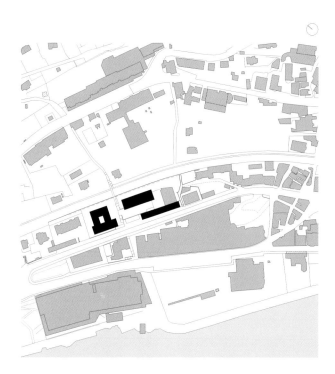

This page: Residential Complex "La Verrière" / aerial view showing north elevation of the complex along the railroad tracks, and proximity of the buildings to the Lake. Opposite, top to bottom: view showing south elevation, and ground floor plans of buildings A, B, and C.

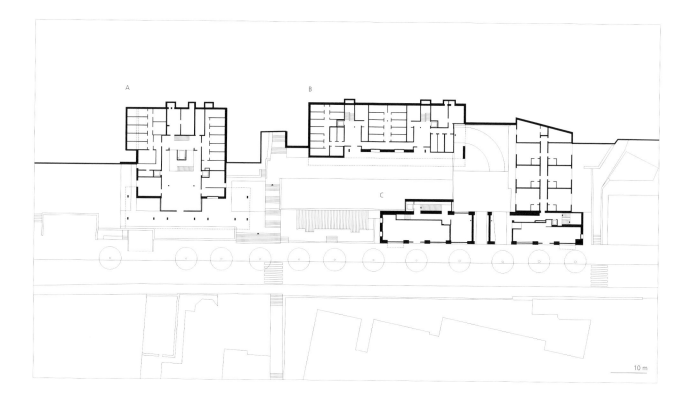

10 m

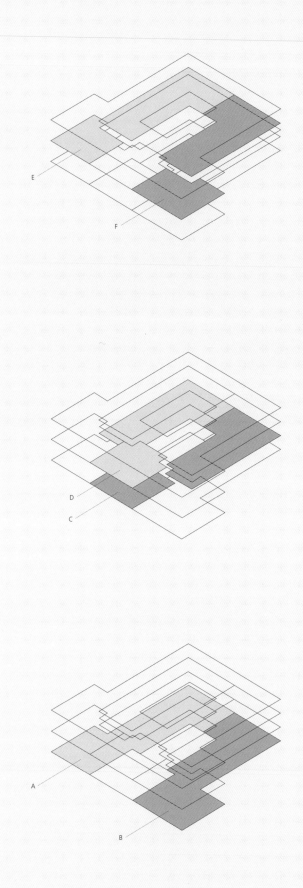

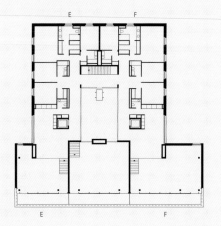

10m

This page: Residential Complex "La Verrière" / interior views showing level changes in various apartment configurations. Opposite page, top to bottom: three plans showing different apartment configurations.

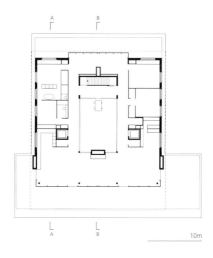

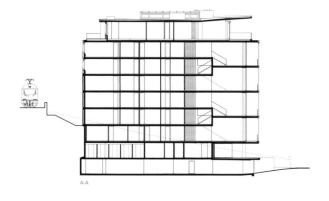

10m

A-A

This page and opposite: Residential Complex "La Verrière" / attic floor plan and section showing level changes inside the different apartment configurations, interior views.

172

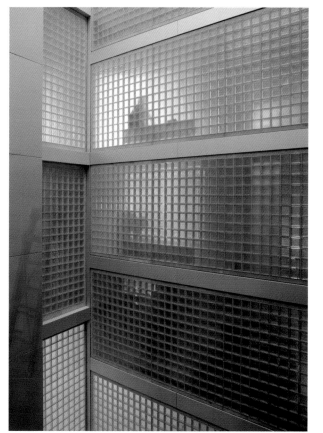

This page and opposite: Residential Complex "La Verrière" / views of central interior courtyard with glass brick, and section through courtyard.

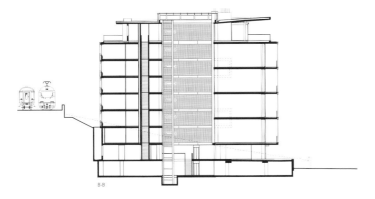

B-B

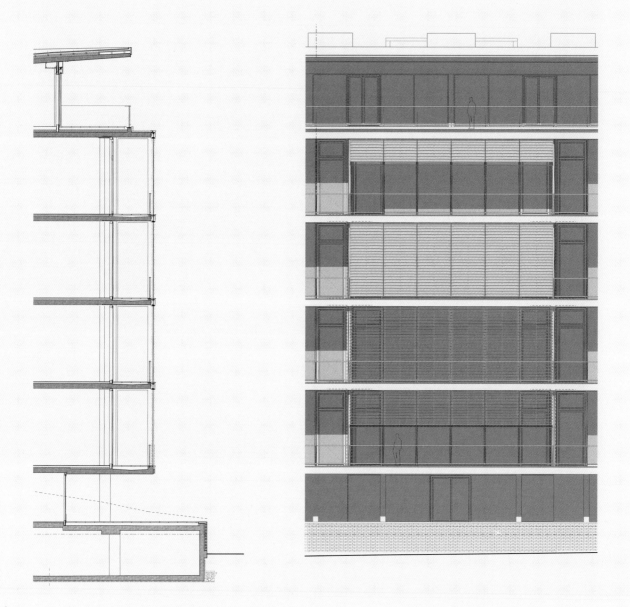

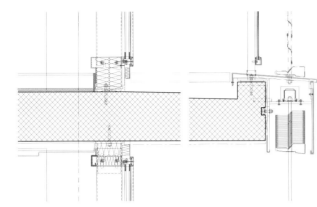

This page, top to bottom: Residential Complex "La Verrière" / construction detail, shade system, and views showing how the facade changes as shades are adjusted to the occupants' needs. Opposite page: detail in section and elevation showing positioning of balcony shade system.

This page and following pages: Residential Complex "La Verrière" / views showing exterior esplanade at the junction of all three buildings, with art installation by Catherine Bolle.

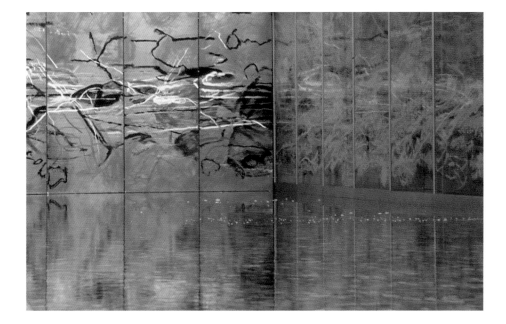

This page, top to bottom: Residential Complex "La Verrière" / aerial view of the complex, and view showing north elevation of building B. Opposite page, left: section through buildings B and C; right, top to bottom: plans of the upper level of duplex apartments on the attic floor, lower level of duplex apartments on sixth floor, typical floor plans (levels 3, 4, and 5), upper level of lofts on second floor, and lower level of lofts on first floor.

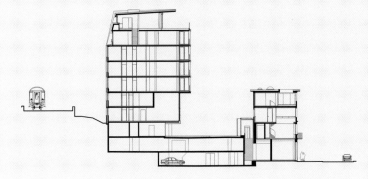

10 m

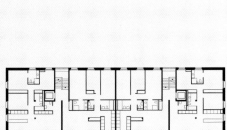

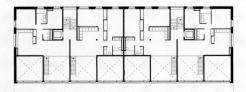

10 m

The New Meeting Place was the second project designed by Richter & Dahl Rocha for IMD's Lausanne campus. This project addresses IMD's goal of enhancing the facilities of its campus for a fast-growing student population. The restaurant and reception hall are located across and downhill from the New Learning Center, and facing Lake Geneva on a level site surrounded by a grove of Centennial trees. The project involved the expansion and renovation of the existing restaurant, a U-shaped masonry building that was once the stable of this private estate. It had already been modestly augmented by the addition of a steel and glass structure, which was replaced by a new pavilion inserted between the two wings of the old building. Not only the Centennial trees, but also abundant vegetation surrounds the pavilion: Toward the lake, the facade gently curves around a mature chestnut tree that has been carefully preserved. Unlike the neighboring New Learning Center, which is elevated above ground and appears as a compact volume looking out over the site, the New Meeting Place maintains a vital connection to the park. A light steel and wood structure, its three facades are composed of large panes of glass supported by vertical structural elements that act as shades while preserving the effect of transparency that the building conveys. The horizontal character of the building is reinforced by the wide roof canopy. Exterior and interior circulation paths begin at an intermediary level to negotiate the natural slope of the terrain. A vertical concrete and brick element at the entrance evokes the solid character of the original building, while concealing a concentration of mechanical systems. The restaurant extends from the ground floor, with its expansive terrace, to the upper floor with views onto the park. Interior spaces express a tension between the strongly vertical wood and glass enclosure and the horizontal thrust of the hung ceiling.

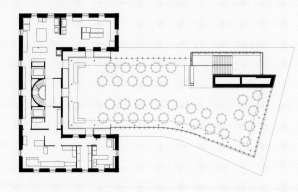

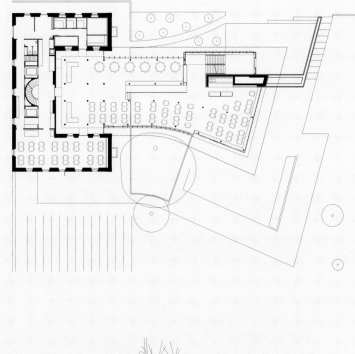

10 m

This page: New Meeting Place, IMD / view showing entrance level above restaurant terrace.
Opposite, top to bottom: plans of second and ground floors, and longitudinal section.

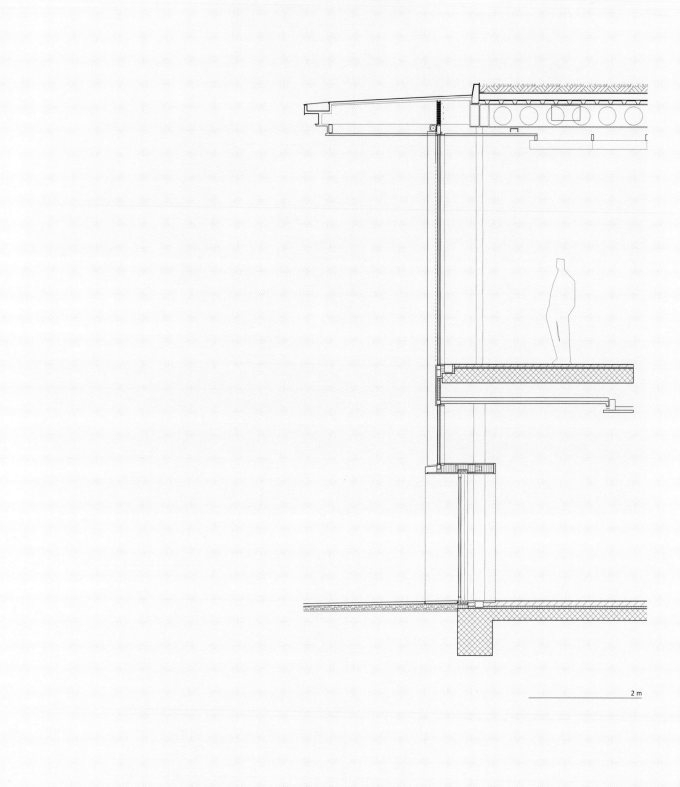

2 m

This page: New Meeting Place, IMD / view of restaurant terrace.
Opposite: construction detail, facade composition.

This page and opposite: New Meeting Place, IMD / interior views.

The pleinAir® Glass Partition System developed and designed for Clestra exemplifies a new form of collaboration between architects, interior designers, and industry. The goal of this new glazed wall system was to achieve the ultimate expression of simplicity and sobriety while allowing maximum flexibility in the integration of modular dividing, shading, screening, and hanging elements with structural framing elements. Of equal importance was their capacity for acoustic performance. The system is essentially comprised of nearly seamless sheets of glass enclosed with minimalist aluminum frames. The glass "skin" can be "doubled" to create an interstitial space capable of accepting various shading or screening materials, and the glass itself can be etched or treated to create different levels of transparency, translucency, and opacity. The search for elegance, clarity of detail, and subtle dimensioning of all elements guided the conception of the pleinAir® system, which was initially driven by more pragmatic objectives such as efficiency and adaptability.

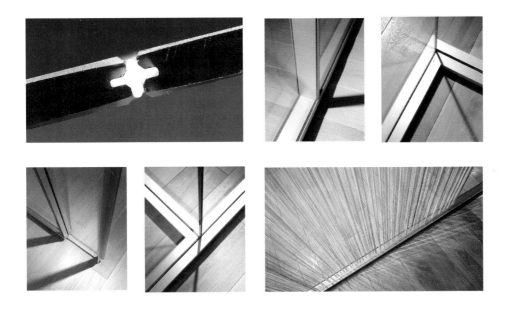

This page: pleinAir® Glass Partition System for Clestra Hauserman SA / views showing possible combinations of pleinAir® partitions. Opposite, top to bottom: construction details in plan and section showing combinations of single or double glass panels, door variants, and detail of extruded aluminum profile in plan and section.

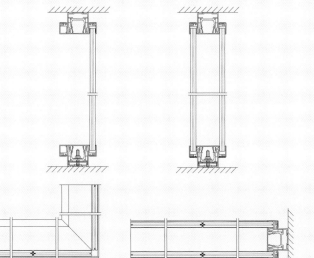
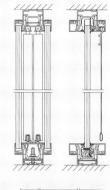
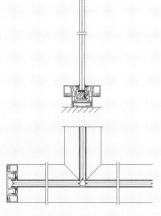

Combinations of glass panels with various shading elements

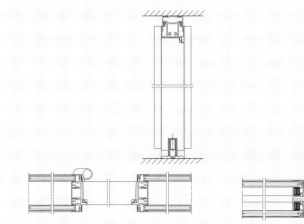
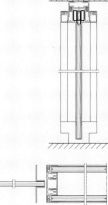
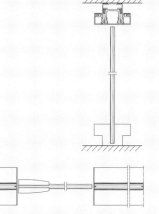

Different door models: hinged plain panel, sliding glass panel, hinged glass

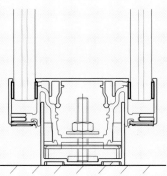
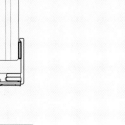
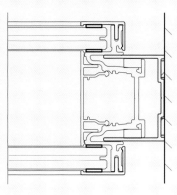

Assembly details

This invited competition held in 2004 consisted of two phases. The first involved the elaboration of a master plan for a complete reorganization of a residential estate at the periphery of Zurich along the road after which the project is named, Im Forster. The second phase was directed toward the development of the residential units themselves. The site is a large, gently sloping parcel offering open views towards the city and the lake of Zurich, the north section of which is occupied by two existing buildings – the client's villa and an adjacent garage. The challenge was to deploy a major residential development around the existing villa without altering the green, almost pastoral character of the estate. The program included a total of 63 dwelling units in seven different apartment buildings, to be divided into three different ensembles: three apartment buildings form what was called the "Mittelberg," located at the southwest end of the parcel, three others were situated at the eastern limit forming the "Gärtnerei," and the last building, comprising four units located closest to the villa, replaced the client's existing "Garage." In order to minimize the impact of new construction on the mature vegetation of this lushly planted site, Richter & Dahl Rocha adopted the following strategy: All apartment buildings would be deployed toward the outer perimeter of the parcel creating a vast park at its center. The volumetric impact of each apartment building was minimized by taking advantage of the uneven topography of the site, utilizing the slope of the terrain to integrate a series of fragmented volumes at varying levels. For the Mittelberg, this strategy was pushed further, so that each of the three units consisted in the juxtaposition of two building typologies: compact volumes evoking a villa typology were articulated above horizontal elements that form terraces extending into the park.

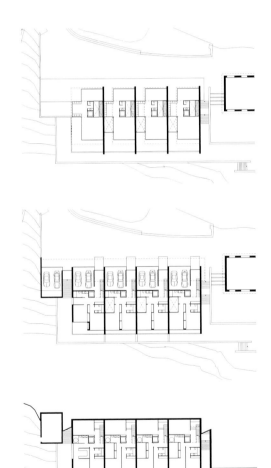

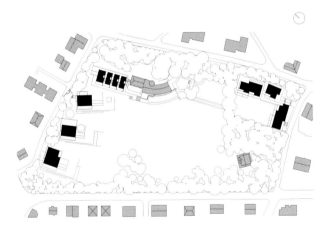

10 m

This page, right top to bottom: Residential Development Im Forster / "Garage" apartment building, plans of upper, ground, and lower-ground floors. Opposite: section, longitudinal section, section, and model.

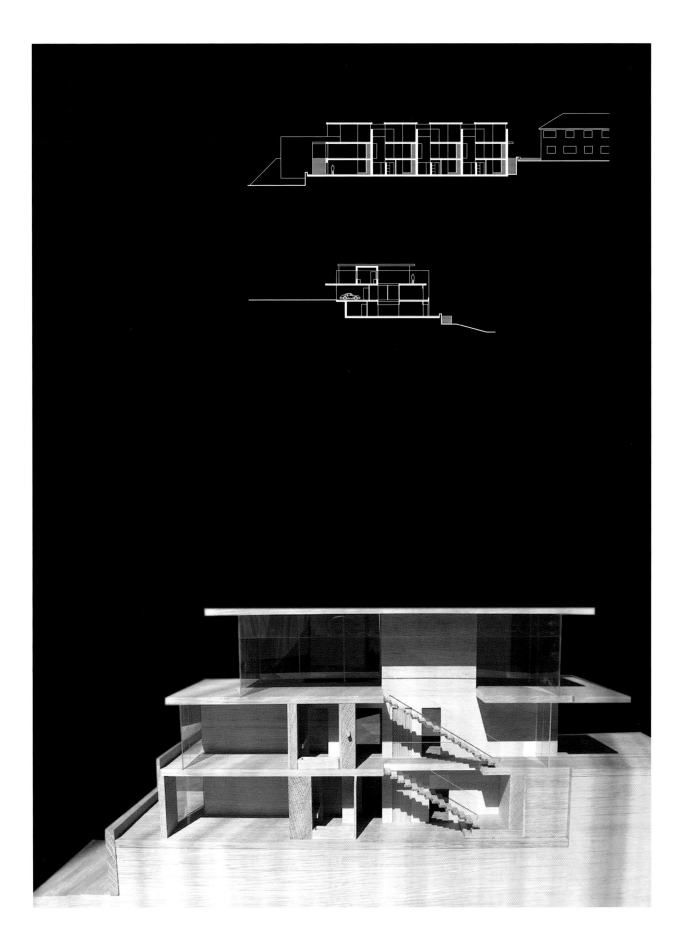

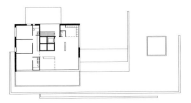

10 m

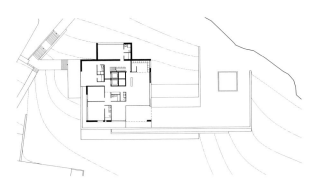

10 m

This page, counterclockwise from upper left: Residential Development Im Forster / "Mittelberg" apartment building, plans of third, second, first, ground, and lower-ground floors, perspective sketch and site plan. Opposite: section showing how the ground and lower-ground floors are integrated into the topography of the site, and model.

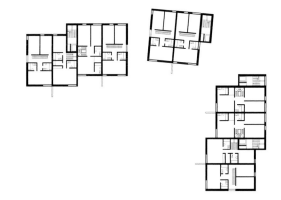

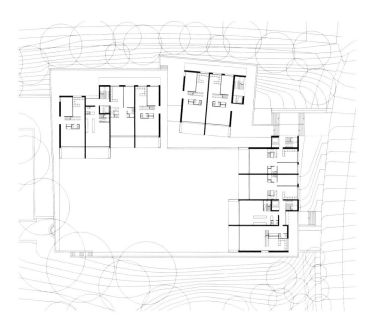

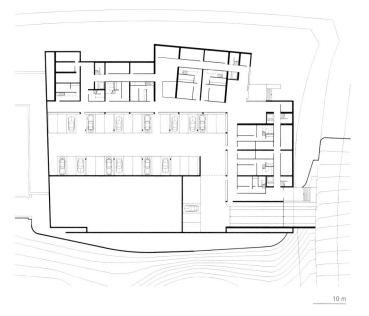

10 m

This page, top to bottom: "Gärtnerei" apartment building, plans of upper, ground, and lower-ground floors.
Opposite: sections, and model.

The site for Lausanne's New Museum of Fine Arts is a trapezoidal parcel fronting on the shore of Lake Geneva, bounded by the General Navigation Company (CGN) shipyard to the east and a historic early modernist pool and beach complex to the west. Although it affords direct access to the lake at its narrow end, the site is compromised by the very different character of its neighboring parcels – an industrial shipyard to one side, and to the other, Marc Piccard's 1937 Bellerive-Plage Pool, which was restored in the early 1990s. Richter & Dahl Rocha proposed a strong gesture to mediate this condition: a very simple bar building facing the lake. Clad in stone and open at both ends, the building rests on a podium that defines the site as a public place. On this new ground, cultural events related to the museum merge with the more spontaneous cultural context generated by pedestrians passing by. In addition to exhibition spaces, the programmatic requirements of the new museum included a reception area and public space, a zone devoted to public education, a conservation area, a library, a museum shop,

a multi-purpose space, and a garden, as well as privately run concessions such as a café and a restaurant. In particular, the positioning of the café at ground level in close proximity to the lake invites visitors to participate in the museum's activities. The main volume of the museum is elevated above ground, and a long staircase leading to an open space overlooking the lake gives access to the various exhibition spaces. At the other end of the building, the facade acts as a large projection screen in dialogue with the city. Designed to free the exhibition spaces of structural elements in order to allow designers and art installers as much flexibility as possible, the building is also equipped with novel systems to facilitate and enhance the display of art works: The roof is composed of a series of sheds oriented to the north which optimize the capture of incoming natural light, and the artificial lighting systems augment this natural source, while translucent glass and horizontal louvers offer various alternatives to accommodate a wide range of curatorial purposes and strategies.

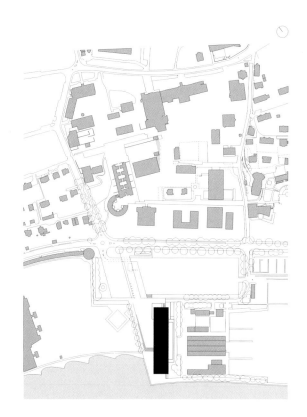

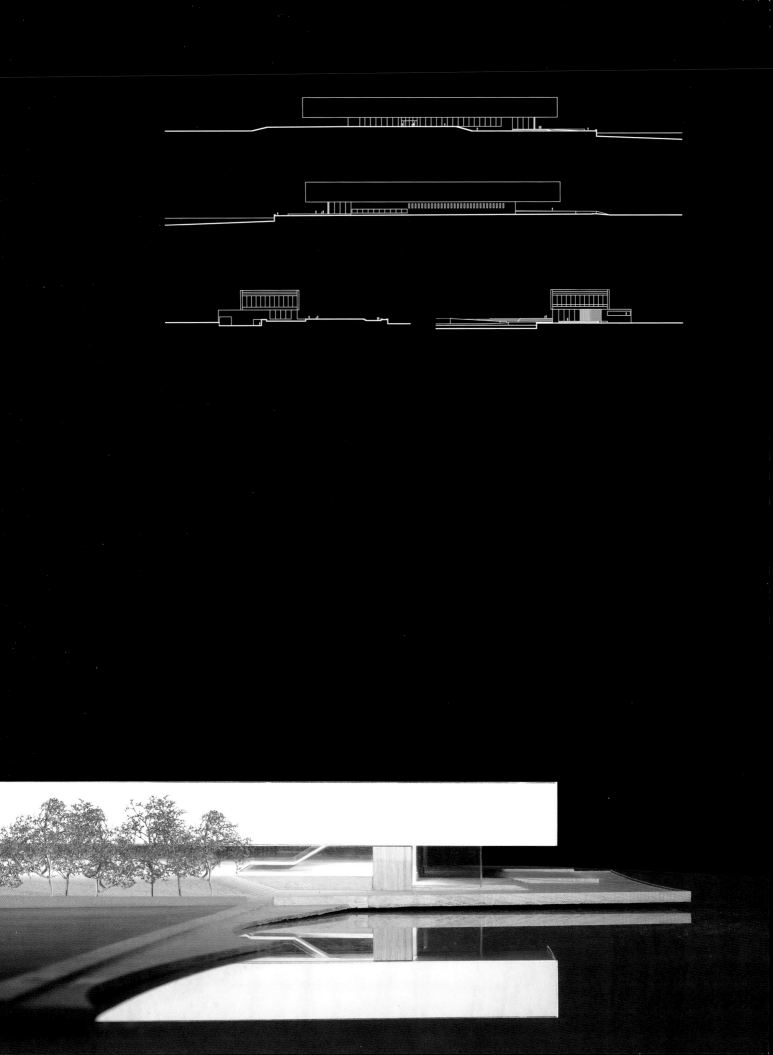

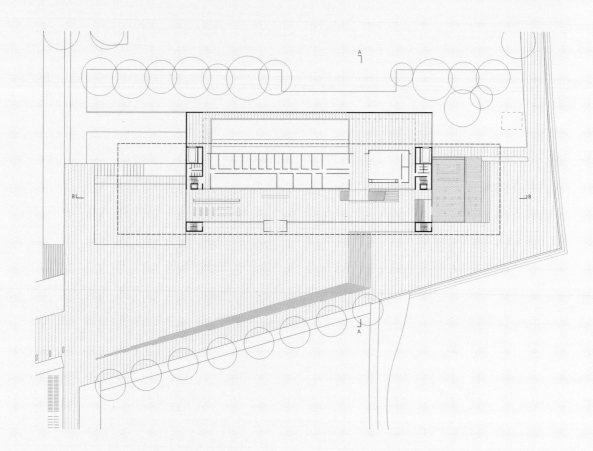

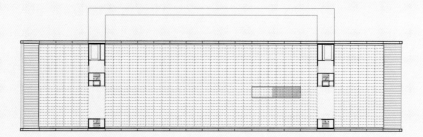

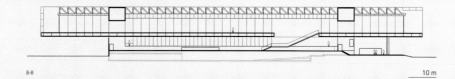

B-B

10 m

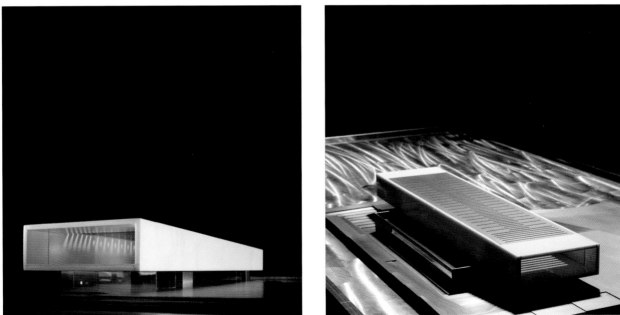

This page: New Museum of Fine Arts / model views.
Opposite, top to bottom: plans of ground and upper floors, and longitudinal section.

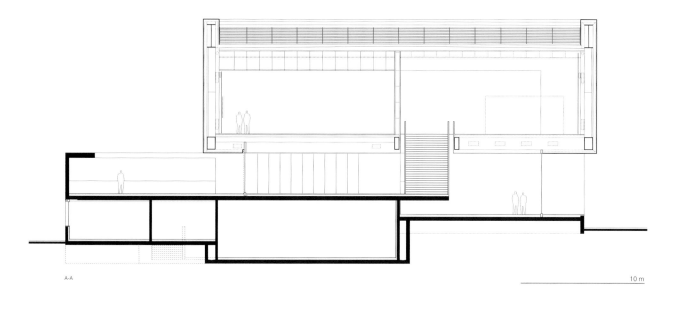

10 m

This page, top to bottom: New Museum of Fine Arts / section through exhibition spaces, and perspective view. Opposite: model views.

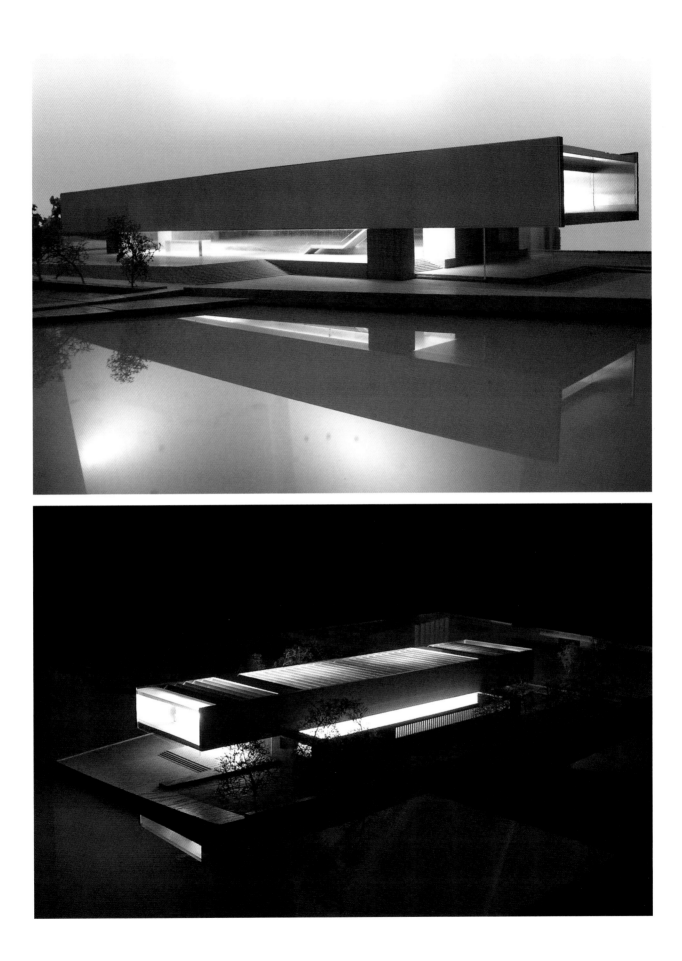

Built between 1911 and 1914, this bank building by archi-tect Eugène Jost with Louis Bezencenet and Maurice Schnell has been owned by the Credit Suisse Group since 1931. The neoclassical edifice, topped by a large cupola, is strategically located in the center of Lausanne, looking out over the city and the lake toward the Alps. In the 1960s, the building was subjected to massive transformations that obliterated certain features of the original interiors. To accommodate current and future functional requirements without compromising the architectural quality of the building, the architects decided to follow a strategy of stripping the interior spaces and floors of the building while preserving and restoring the facades. By enclosing an indentation on the east facade of the building, Richter & Dahl Rocha created a glazed interior volume that houses a new staircase providing access to public spaces on the upper floors. The Credit Suisse program included teller windows, offices for client meetings on the mezzanine and second floors, two floors of private office spaces, and a public area on the sixth floor, with a new circular conference room centered beneath the carefully restored cupola. The new pre-cast plaster ceiling of the ground floor hall follows the arcuated form of the original neoclassical windows. Moving from the outer wall, where each arched window is framed by a canopied vault, the ceiling flattens out as it moves inward, becoming a perfectly level surface at the mezzanine. This contemporary gesture simultaneously restores a lost original element of the historic building and invokes the modernist "hung" ceiling.

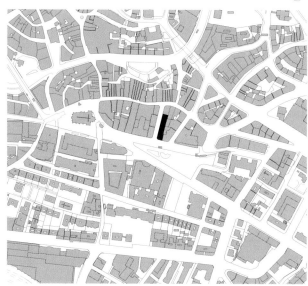

Previous page: Credit Suisse Regional Headquarters / view of main public hall with vaulted ceiling. This page: interior views. Opposite: axonometric views of ground, fifth, and sixth floors, and canopied vaulting of pre-cast plaster ceiling above ground floor hall.

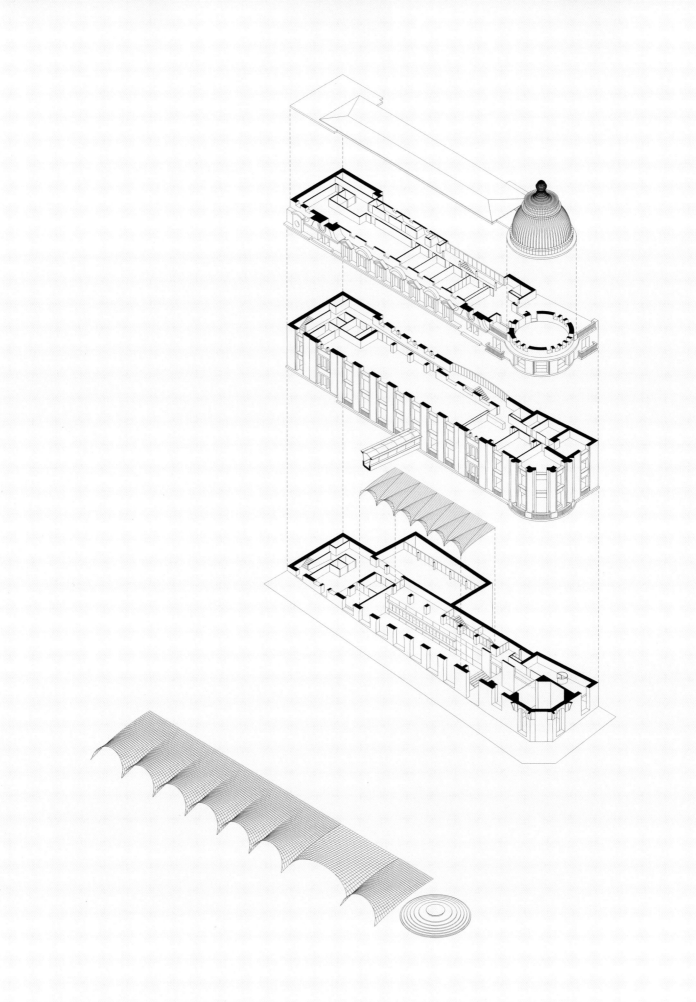

This project for the newly renovated Nestlé Headquarters was motivated by the company's desire to replace the existing dining facilities and to provide its collaborators with a new restaurant and other amenities representative of the company's vision and leading position in the nutrition industry. Located at the east end of the lakefront site, the new building's position, as well as the landscape design associated with the project, extend the park toward the east. This positioning was intended to preserve and extend the most striking part of the site. The top floor houses a restaurant and kitchen, and the ground floor, a cafeteria with food preparation areas. At the lower ground level are meeting and gathering rooms in addition to a gym and a small medical center. Echoing the curved form of Tschumi's Y-shaped building, the new restaurant's circular shape and glass curtain facade – completely open to the surrounding site – creates optimum conditions for circulation and takes advantage of the spectacular views. All of the tables are oriented toward the perimeter of the restaurant, and thus capture views toward the park, the lake, and the Alps in the distant background. At the heart of the building, an ample spiral staircase invokes Tschumi's double-spiral "Chambord" staircase as it connects all three levels. Two staircases and an elevator complete the circulation scheme. Concrete pillars that support exposed concrete slabs and the broad metal roof canopy contribute equally to the essentially contemporary architectural expression of the building, at the same time paying homage to Tschumi's original project.

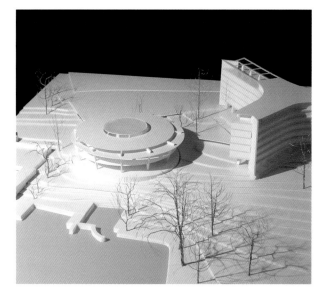

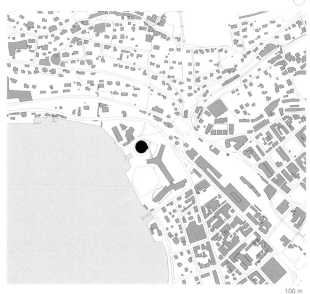

100 m

Opposite page, top to bottom: : Nestlé Headquarters Restaurant and WellNes Center / plans of upper and ground floors, and section.

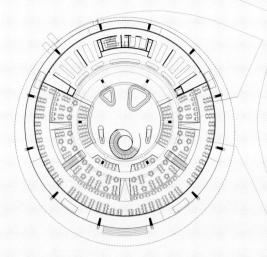

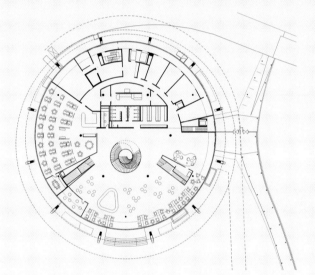

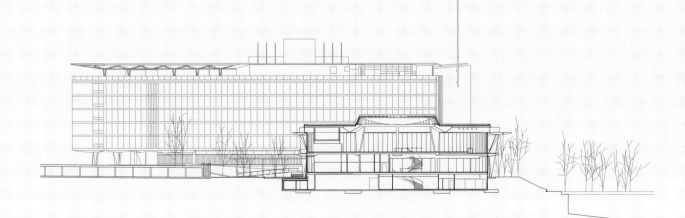

10m

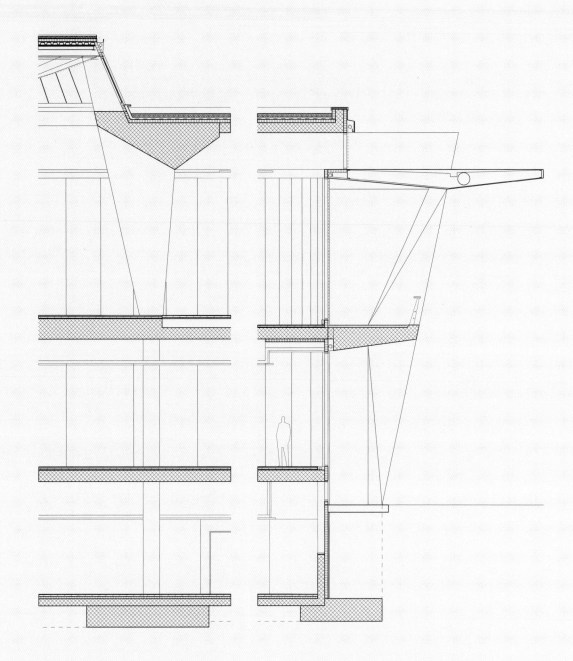

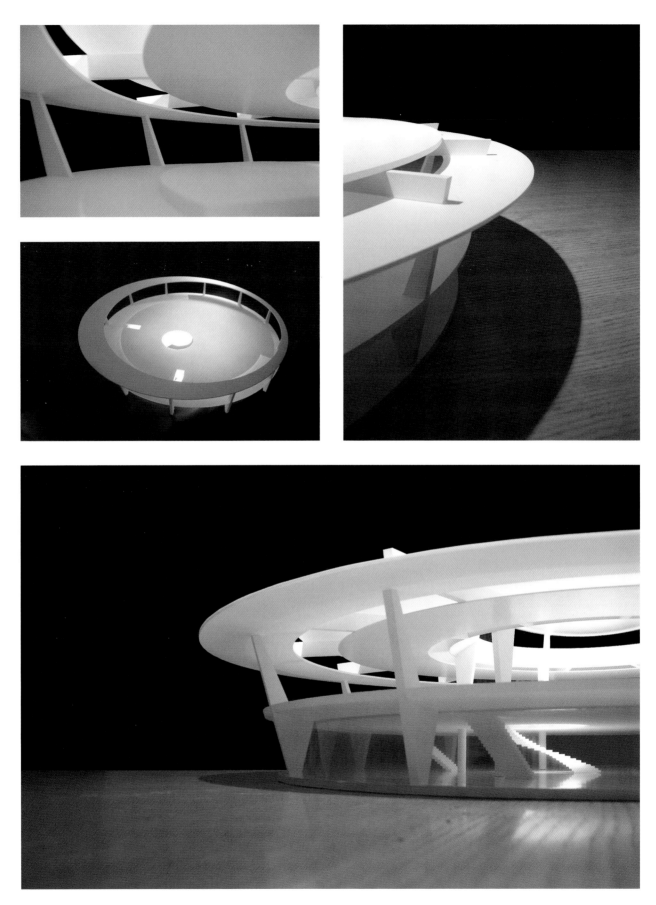

This page: Nestlé Headquarters Restaurant and WellNes Center / model views. Opposite: section showing structural and glass curtain wall systems.

Located in the old industrial zone at the heart of Lausanne, at the southwest end of the quarter known as "Le Flon," this project adopts an urban strategy which is closely related to that of Richter & Dahl Rocha's "Flon-Ville" competition entry. Here, the architects were asked to develop a facade concept appropriate to the commercial purpose of the project by clearly expressing the presence of a large underground shopping complex. The program was broken into four distinct volumes, which in plan follow the perimeters of demolished warehouse buildings that once occupied the site. The larger one to the north is entirely dedicated to commercial purposes, while the other three house various functions: commercial activities at ground level, offices, and even apartments in two of the attic floors. Though this "fragmentation" invokes the building typologies most characteristic of Le Flon, Richter & Dahl Rocha's architectural language clashes with exiting warehouses, which for the most part comprise masonry walls pierced by small windows. Striving for the purest and most abstract form, each simple glass volume has a clarity that is heightened by its constructive details. The

connection between facade and roof is treated as a continuous glass surface for the north building, while for the three other volumes, the vertical windows that open toward the inside for natural ventilation are masked on the exterior by lightweight aluminum sheets aligned with the glazed facade, giving it a more abstract and less tectonic character.

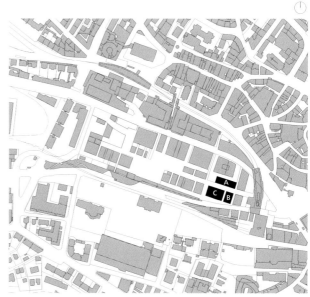

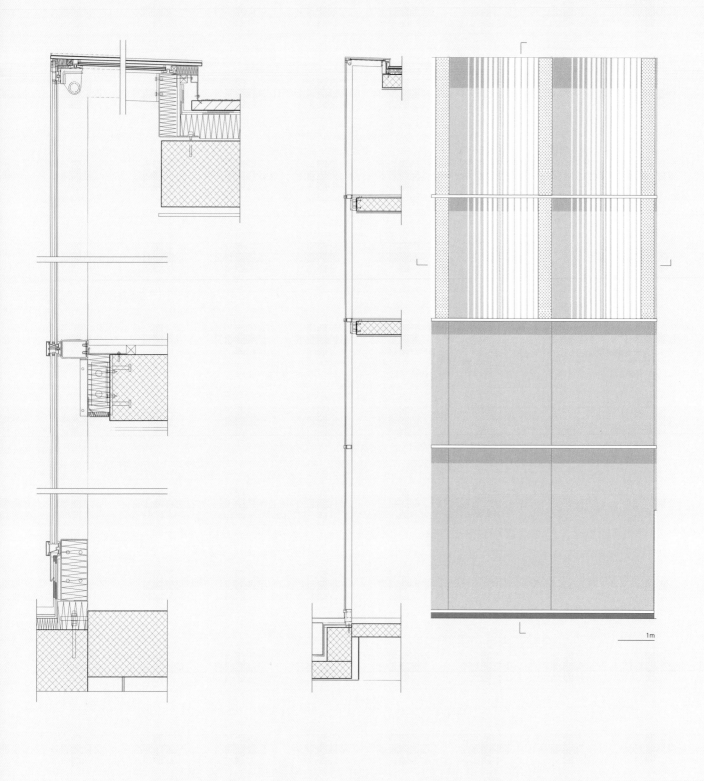

1m

0.50 m

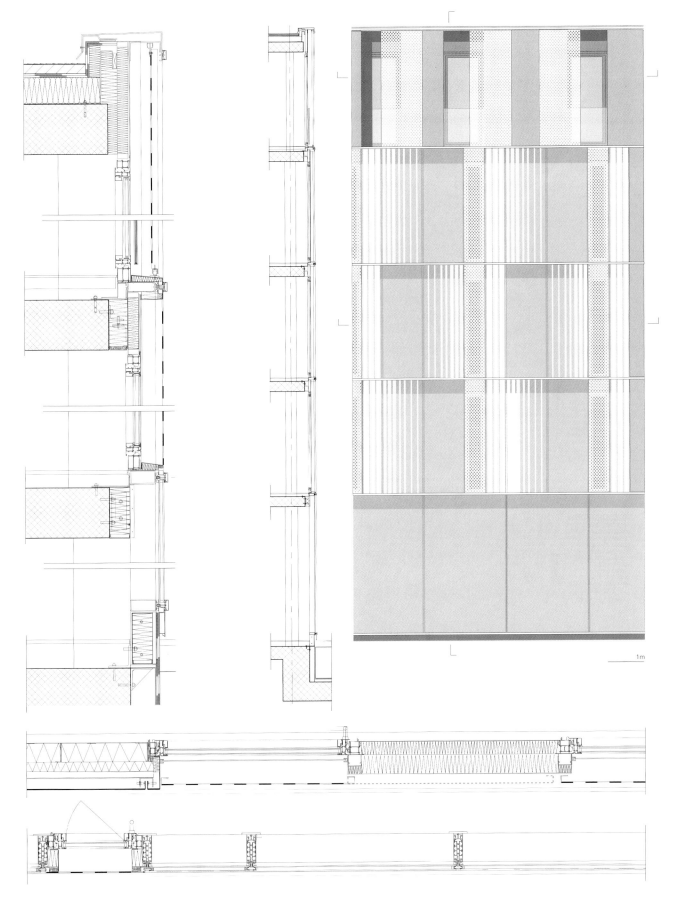

0.50 m

1m

This page: Flon Les Mercier / construction details in plan, section, and elevation, facades for commercial, office, and apartment buildings. Opposite: construction details in plan, section, and elevation, facade for shopping complex.

221

This page, top to bottom: Golay Buchel & Cie Headquarters, and Energie de l'Ouest Suisse (EOS) Headquarters, Lausanne.

ADMINISTRATIVE BUILDINGS

2001–06   CREDIT SUISSE REGIONAL HEADQUARTERS / Renovation & Transformation
Lausanne, Switzerland

2001–05   OFFICE BUILDING AT ROUTE DE BERNE 46
Lausanne, Switzerland

2001–03   CRÉDIT AGRICOLE SUISSE SA / Extension of Logistic Center
Lausanne, Switzerland

1999–2000   VILLA LA FALAISE / Renovation & Expansion for UEFA
Nyon, Switzerland

1996–2000   NESTLÉ HEADQUARTERS / Renovation & Transformation
Vevey, Switzerland

1999   RICHTER & DAHL ROCHA OFFICE / Renovation & Expansion
Lausanne, Switzerland

1997–98   "LES UTTINS" / Project for three administrative buildings
Rolle, Switzerland

1993–95   OFFICE BUILDING AT VALENTIN 10 / Transformation
Lausanne, Switzerland

1991–97   GOLAY BUCHEL & CIE HEADQUARTERS
Lausanne, Switzerland

1991–95   ÉNERGIE DE L'OUEST SUISSE (EOS) HEADQUARTERS
Lausanne, Switzerland

1987–92   BCV BANKING ADMINISTRATIVE CENTER, LEARNING CENTER & RESTAURANT
In association with Suter & Suter, Prilly, Switzerland

This page: St-Antoine Commercial Center, Vevey.

COMMERCIAL & INDUSTRIAL BUILDINGS

2005–08   FLON LES MERCIER / Facade Concept
Lausanne, Switzerland

1999–2005   ST-ANTOINE COMMERCIAL CENTER / Renovation & Transformation
Vevey, Switzerland

1987–2006   C&A MODE BRENNINKMEIJER & CIE /
Transformation & Refurbishing of commercial buildings
Zurich, Lausanne, Geneva, Sion, La Chaux-de-Fonds, Switzerland

2003   WATCH MANUFACTURING PLANT NOUVELLE LÉMANIA BRÉGUET /
Preliminary Design
Le Chenit, Switzerland

2002–03   NESTLÉ PRODUCT TECHNOLOGY CENTER /
Development Plant & Offices
Singen, Germany

2001–02   IKEA STORE
Aubonne, Switzerland

2000–01   NESTLÉ PRODUCT TECHNOLOGY CENTER / Transformation
Orbe, Switzerland

1999–2001   NESTLÉ PRODUCT TECHNOLOGY CENTER / Extension & Transformation
Konolfingen, Switzerland

1999–2000   INDUSTRIAL AND ADMINISTRATION BUILDING FOR KYBURZ / Project
Marin-Épagnier, Switzerland

1995–99   SWISS NATIONAL TRAIN MAINTENANCE CENTER
Geneva Station, Switzerland

1994–96   MANUFACTURING PLANT FOR PKL COMBIBLOC ASIA LTD / Project
Rayong, Thailand

1994–95   INTERNATIONAL EXHIBITION CENTER AND HOTEL "VEFAC EXPO-HOTEL" / Project
Hanoi, Vietnam

1994–95   GLASS BOTTLE FACTORY / Project
Jebel-ali, Arab Emirates

1991–95   JUMBO SHOPPING MALL / Extension & Transformation
Villars-sur-Glâne, Switzerland

This page, top to bottom: Villa Zbar, Lausanne, and Shamrock apartment building, Pully.

HOUSING

2004–09	RESIDENTIAL DEVELOPMENT IN AUBONNE / 2 Apartment buildings with 72 units Aubonne, Switzerland
2003–09	BEAU SÉJOUR 8 / Apartment building with 125 units Lausanne, Switzerland
2005–07	RESIDENTIAL DEVELOPMENT "LES UTTINS"/ Apartment building G with 37 units Rolle, Switzerland
2004–08	CHERNEX / Apartment building with 7 units Montreux, Switzerland
2002–05	RESIDENTIAL DEVELOPMENT "LES UTTINS"/ Apartment building F with 28 units Rolle, Switzerland
2001–05	RESIDENTIAL COMPLEX "LA VERRIÈRE" / 2 Apartment buildings with 46 units, & renovation of existing apartment building and commercial spaces Montreux, Switzerland
2002–03	TREYBLANC LA BÂLOISE / Renovation of 50 apartments Lausanne, Switzerland
1999–2003	RESIDENTIAL DEVELOPMENT "LES UTTINS"/ Apartment building E with 18 units Rolle, Switzerland
1999–2008	VILLA SAGER Jeddah, Saudi Arabia
1999–2000	VILLA ZBAR Lausanne, Switzerland
1998–2002	RESIDENTIAL DEVELOPMENT "LES UTTINS"/ Apartment building D with 25 units Rolle, Switzerland
1997–2000	SWHome® VALMONT / 10 Townhouses Lausanne, Switzerland
1996–97	SHAMROCK / Apartment building with 7 units Pully, Switzerland
1995–96	SWHome® TWIN VILLAS Chailly, Switzerland
1992–95	STE-LUCE & GROTTE / Apartment building with 10 units, & commercial spaces Lausanne, Switzerland
1991–95	RESIDENTIAL DEVELOPMENT IN PRILLY / Apartment building with 757 units Prilly, Switzerland
1988–95	SWHome® HOUSING SYSTEM / Study for the development of modular & flexible housing units

This page: International School of Geneva (EIG). Opposite: Grange-Verney School of Agriculture.

EDUCATION

2006–08 LES BOIS CHAMBLARD / Renovation & Transformation of a
villa for the École Polytechnique Fédérale, Lausanne (EPFL)
Buchillon, Switzerland

2005–08 NEW CENTER FOR CREATIVE LEARNING, IMD
Lausanne, Switzerland

2004–06 NEW RESEARCH CENTER, IMD
Lausanne, Switzerland

2002–05 NEW MEETING PLACE, IMD / Restaurant & Conference Center
Lausanne, Switzerland

1999–2002 NEW LEARNING CENTER, IMD
Lausanne, Switzerland

2000 INTERNATIONAL SCHOOL OF GENEVA (EIG) / Project
Geneva, Switzerland

1996–2001 VALMONT BOARDING SCHOOL / Extension
Lausanne, Switzerland

1995–96 VALMONT BOARDING SCHOOL / Transformation
Lausanne, Switzerland

1989–90 GRANGE-VERNEY SCHOOL OF AGRICULTURE / Project
Grange-Verney, Switzerland

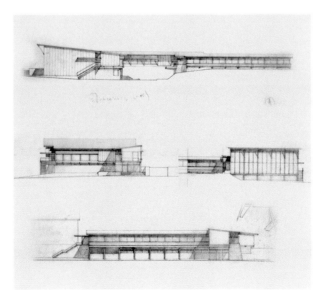

This page: Contemporary Art Museum FAE, Prilly.

URBANISM

2006   PSE-SCIENCE PARK / Urban Planning for the
               École Polytechnique Fédérale, Lausanne (EPFL)
               Écublens, Switzerland

2004   CITY HALL "FLON-VILLE" / Competition
               Lausanne, Switzerland

1994–96   AU PRÉ-DU-CANAL / Urban Development Project
               Yverdon-les-Bains, Switzerland

1993   GARE CRÊT-TACONNET / Urban Development Project
               Neuchâtel, Switzerland

1993   SI BELLE CROIX / study for urban renewal & development of new urban node
               Villars-sur-Glâne, Switzerland

1992–94   LES CÈDRES / Urban Development Project with apartment buildings
               & commercial spaces
               Chavannes-près-Renens, Switzerland

1987–94   ESPACITÉ / Administrative, Commercial, & Residential Complex
               La Chaux-de-Fonds, Switzerland

OTHER PROJECTS

2005–09   PARK & RIDE VENNES-AQUAÉCOPÔLE / Parking Lot with 1200 places
               connected to the M2 subway station, Hotel with 120 rooms, Medical Center,
               & Fresh Water Museum & Theme Park
               Lausanne, Switzerland

2005–08   NESTLÉ HEADQUARTERS RESTAURANT & WELLNES CENTER
               Vevey, Switzerland

2001–05   LA PRAIRIE CLINIC / Extension & Transformation
               Clarens-Montreux, Switzerland

2003–04   NESTLÉ HEADQUARTERS / Restaurant Transformation
               Vevey, Switzerland

1996   NOTARY PUBLIC OFFICE & THEATER
               Pully, Switzerland

1993–95   PROTOTYPE FOR A FOREST REFUGE
               "La Racine," Grand Risoux Forest, Canton Vaud, Switzerland

1990–91   CONTEMPORARY ART MUSEUM FAE / Transformation of an existing building
               for Fondation Asher Edelman, Pully, Switzerland

This page, top to bottom: Park & Ride Vennes-AquaÉcopôle, Lausanne, and World Intellectual Property Organization (WIPO) Headquarters, Geneva.

SELECTED COMPETITIONS

2006
Invited Competition / Finalists
KARL STEINER HEADQUARTERS / New Facade Concept
& Renovation of ground floor
Zurich, Switzerland

2005
Invited Competition
FONDATION RIVE-NEUVE / Clinic
Blonay, Switzerland

2005
Invited Proposal / First Prize
PARK & RIDE VENNES-AQUAÉCOPÔLE
Lausanne, Switzerland

2004–05
International Competition / Fifth Prize
NEW MUSEUM OF FINE ARTS
Lausanne, Switzerland

2004
Invited Competition / Third Prize
RESIDENTIAL DEVELOPMENT IM FORSTER
Zurich, Switzerland

2004
Invited Competition / Finalists
OLYMPIC INTERNATIONAL COMMITTEE (CIO) / Extension
Lausanne, Switzerland

2003
Invited Competition / Forth Prize
"FLON-VILLE" CITY HALL
Lausanne, Switzerland

2002
Invited Competition / Finalists
MANOR / Shopping Mall
Bienne/Biel, Switzerland

2002
Invited Competition
TÉLÉVERBIER "MÉDRAN" / Hotel & Apartment Buildings
Verbier, Switzerland

2001
Invited Competition
CHAMP-CHAMOT / Residential Development
Belmont, Switzerland

2001
International Competition
ZURICH AIRPORT
Zurich, Switzerland

2000
International Competition / Third Prize
WORLD INTELLECTUAL PROPERTY ORGANIZATION (WIPO) / Extension
Geneva, Switzerland

2000
International Competition / Second Prize
INTERNATIONAL SCHOOL OF GENEVA (EIG)
Geneva, Switzerland

1996
Invited Competition / First Prize
CREDIT SUISSE REGIONAL HEADQUARTERS / Renovation & Transformation
Lausanne, Switzerland

1991
Invited Competition / First Prize
ÉNERGIE DE L'OUEST SUISSE (EOS) / Headquarters
Lausanne, Switzerland

1990
Invited Competition / Second Prize
AGY-FRIBOURG / Administrative Building, Conference Center, & Technical Park
Fribourg, Switzerland

1990
National Competition / First Prize
AVANCHES SPORTS & LEISURE COMPLEX
Avenches, Switzerland

1989
International Competition / Entry Prize
FIRST EUROPAN COMPETITION ON HOUSING
Switzerland

1987
National Competition / First Prize
URBAN RENEWAL PROJECT
La Chaux-de-Fonds, Switzerland

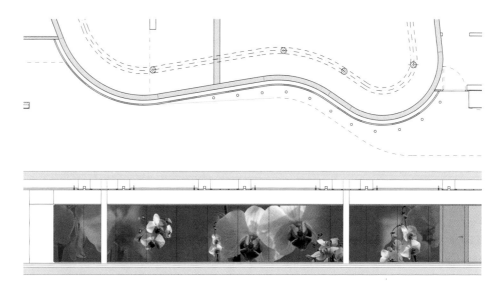

This page, top to bottom: chair and curving wall covered in custom-designed silk, main dining room, La Prairie Clinic, Clarens-Montreux.

RDR DESIGN SA

2006–08   NESTLÉ HEADQUARTERS RESTAURANT & WELLNES CENTER /
Interior Design
Vevey, Switzerland

2006   VILLA SAGER / Interior Design & Furnishings
Jeddah, Saudi Arabia

2006   NESTLÉ SUISSE / Interior Design of Nestlé Company Store &
Landscape Design
La-Tour-de-Peilz, Switzerland

2005–06   NESTLÉ SUISSE / Interior Design of Swiss Headquarters
La-Tour-de-Peilz, Switzerland

2005   NEW MEETING PLACE, IMD / Spatial Study & Furnishings
Lausanne, Switzerland

2004–05   LA PRAIRIE CLINIC / Interior Design, Custom Furniture,
Signage & Corporate Identity
Lausanne, Switzerland

2004–05   CLESTRA HAUSERMAN SA / Showroom Design
Strasbourg, France

2004–05   pleinAir® GLASS PARTITION SYSTEM FOR
CLESTRA HAUSERMAN SA (Strasbourg)
Lausanne, Switzerland

2003   NESTLÉ HEADQUARTERS / Landscape Design
Vevey, Switzerland

2001–05   CRÉDIT AGRICOLE SUISSE / Interior Design of private banking spaces
Lausanne, Lugano, Zurich, Basel & Geneva, Switzerland

1998–2000   CUSTOM FURNITURE DESIGNS FOR HUGHES CHEVALIER INC. (PARIS)
Lausanne, Switzerland

2002   NESTLÉ HEADQUARTERS COMPANY STORE / Facade Concept
& Interior Design
Vevey, Switzerland

2002   VRIJSEN APARTMENT / Interior Design
Rolle, Switzerland

RICHTER & DAHL ROCHA ARCHITECTS

Jacques Richter was born in Lausanne in 1954 and studied architecture at the Swiss Federal Institute of Technology (ETH) in Zurich from 1974 to 1979. He received his diploma in 1979 and entered the postgraduate program at the Yale School of Architecture in 1981, completing the MArch degree in 1983. After working as an associate in the firm of Max Richter and Marcel Gut from 1983 to 1992, he established Richter & Dahl Rocha Architects in Lausanne in 1993 with Ignacio Dahl Rocha, whom he had met at Yale. Richter has taught at the École d'architecture Athenaeum in Lausanne (EAAL) from 1984 to 1989. President of the Lausanne Jardins landscape architecture festival (2004 & 2009), he also presided over the FAR Forum d'Architecture Romande in 2005, headed the board of the Quatrième Distinction Vaudoise d'Architecture from 1995 to 1997, and from 1991 to 1998, served as president of the board of the dance company Philippe Saire in Lausanne.

Ignacio Dahl Rocha was born in Buenos Aires, Argentina, in 1956 and studied architecture at the University of Buenos Aires from 1973 to 1978. He received his diploma in 1979 and entered the postgraduate program at the Yale School of Architecture in 1981. He completed the MArch degree in 1983, receiving the Excellence in Architecture Prize. Between 1983 and 1989, Dahl Rocha practiced architecture as a principal of the firm Billoch, Dahl Rocha, Ramos Arquitectos. Since 1990, he has been living and working in Lausanne, Switzerland, where he established Richter & Dahl Rocha Architects in 1993 with Jacques Richter. Dahl Rocha taught at the Harvard University Graduate School of Design in 2000 and has lectured at various universities in Europe, the United States and Latin America, including Yale University, the University of Buenos Aires, the University Simón Bolívar in Caracas in Venezuela, and the Catholic University of Santiago, Chile. In 2001, he received the Premio Vitruvio for his career as a Latin American architect.

Kenneth Ross was born in Buenos Aires in 1964 and studied architecture at the University of Buenos Aires from 1983 to 1989. He received his diploma in 1989 and joined Richter and Dahl Rocha in Lausanne a year later. He has been an associate of the firm since 1996, heading such key commissions as the renovation and transformation of the Nestlé Headquarters in Vevey, the Nestlé Product Technology Center in Singen, Germany, and the office building at Route de Berne 46 in Lausanne.

Christian Leibbrandt was born in Basel in 1954 and studied architecture at the École Polytechnique Fédérale Lausanne (EPFL) from 1974 to 1979, obtaining his diploma in 1980. In 1987, he entered a joint graduate program of the EPFL and the University of Buenos Aires to pursue doctoral research on processes of "self-construction," completing his dissertation in 1992. In 1993, Leibbrandt joined Richter & Dahl Rocha Architects in Lausanne and became an associate in 1996. He headed major projects such as the urban development plan for housing and commercial buildings "Les Uttins," the extension of the La Prairie Clinic in Montreux, and the development project for Au Pré-du-Canal.

Manuel Perez was born in Sober (Lugo), Spain, in 1959 and studied architecture at the Geneva School of Engineers (EIG) from 1977 to 1980, completing his diploma in 1980. In 1992, he joined Richter and Dahl Rocha in Lausanne, where he acted as site manager for several commissions, including the Golay-Buchel Headquarters in Lausanne, the renovation and transformation of the Nestlé Headquarters in Vevey, and the extension of the La Prairie Clinic in Montreux. Perez has worked as a team manager for Richter & Dahl Rocha Architects since 2005.

RDR DESIGN SA

Cédric Simon was born in Lausanne in 1970. He completed a draftsman's apprenticeship in 1991 and pursued his architectural education at the Technical Superior School of Lugano Trevano and at the École d'ingénieurs et d'architectes de Fribourg (EIF). He obtained his diploma in 1997. The same year, he joined Richter & Dahl Rocha in Lausanne, working primarily on furniture and interior design projects in the context of the renovation and transformation of the Nestlé Headquarters in Vevey. In 2002, Simon assumed responsibility as team manager for the newly created RDR design SA, an associated firm that specializes in design commissions ranging from interior design, custom furniture and visual communication to projects of industrial design developed in collaboration with industry manufacturers such as the pleinAir® Glass Partition System for Clestra or the custom-designed living room ensemble for Hughes Chevalier.

RICHTER-DAHL ROCHA Y ASOCIADOS, ARGENTINA

Barbara Moyano Gacitúa was born in Buenos Aires in 1973 and studied architecture at the University of Buenos Aires as well as at the École Polytechnique Fédérale, Lausanne (EPFL) from 1994 to 2002, obtaining her diploma in 2003. In 1998, after winning a scholarship in the context of a seminar organized at the Universidad di Tella in Buenos Aires, she joined Richter & Dahl Rocha Architects, where she has been a project manager since 2003. After heading projects such as the New Meeting Place for the International Institute for Management Development (IMD) in Lausanne, in 2006, upon returning to Argentina, Barbara Moyano Gacitúa collaborated with Bruno Emmer on the creation of Richter-Dahl Rocha y Asociados.

Bruno Emmer was born in Buenos Aires in 1973 and studied architecture at the University of Buenos Aires from 1992 to 1998, obtaining his diploma in 1998. Before joining Richter & Dahl Rocha Architects in 1999, he collaborated with Lerner, Dellatorre, Shanahan Architects, as well as architect Pablo Doval in Buenos Aires. Emmer's involvement at Richter & Dahl Rocha has included the preliminary residential projects for "La Verrière" and "Les Uttins." He also acted as project manager for the extension of the La Prairie Clinic in Montreux. In 2006, he returned to Buenos Aires, where with Barbara Moyano Gacitúa he collaborated on the creation of Richter-Dahl Rocha y Asociados.

RICHTER & DAHL ROCHA

Jacques Richter
Ignacio Dahl Rocha
Kenneth Ross
Christian Leibbrandt
Manuel Perez
Hicham Amia
Adrien Barakat
Antoine Barc
Johannes Beaujolin
Nicolas Braem
Mauro Branco
Mark Chaille
Diego Comamala
Frédéric Comby
Maxime Duvoisin
Bernard Emonet
Christophe Gachnang
Christian Gonin
Pouska Haessig
Martin Ioelster
Miroslav Jandejsek
Alain Jaquenod
Baris Kansu
Nathalie Khelfi
Roberto Kossi Odi
Carine Lombardi
Maria Losana Vela
Martin Mouzo
Hector Nunez
Michel Paganin
Santiago Pagés
Fabrice Roulin
Philippe Schmittler
Manuela Toscan
Giancarlo Troccoli
Thanh-Tung Trinh
Bruno Tschudi
Olivier Wavre
Alexis Wintsch

ADMINISTRATION

Isabelle Simon
Julia Bassetti
Simone Chardon
Alexandra Desvoignes
Catarina Filipe
Anne-Sylvie Isely
Marijana Lucic

RDR DESIGN

Cédric Simon
Claudia Dell'Ariccia
Juliane Mayor
Marco Turin
Konstantin Tzonis
Patrick Winterhalter

**RICHTER-DAHL ROCHA
Y ASOCIADOS**

Bruno Emmer
Barbara Moyano Gacitúa
Valentina Cambiaso
Delfina Degliantoni
Bruno Osvaldo Goroni

MODEL MAKERS

Aurel Aebi
Yves Gigon
René Jeanneret
Marc Menoud
Patrick Reymond

FORMER EMPLOYEES

Katia Amendola
Hüsseyn Araz
Antoine Baillie
Sophie Beaubien
Philippe Beboux
Diego Behrend
Stéphanie Bender
Carole Berset
Claude-Alain Bieri
Francisco Billoch
Félix Blum
Barbara Boni
Olivier Bottarelli
Cornelius Boy
Patrick Burgy
Cecilia Carena
Isabella Carpiceci Hahne
Edson Cayana
Denis Clermont
Samanta Cornolti
Sylvie Costa

Vincent Costa
Antonio Da Silva
Bautista Dahl Rocha
Guillermo Dahl Rocha
Xavier Depeursinge
Lucienne Di Biase Dooley
Enrico Di Giuseppe
Caroline Dionne
Pablo Doval
Thierry Duvoisin
Silvia Fernandes C.
Patrick Gaberel
Christian Galvao
Chrystel Ganty
Pierre Gervais
Renaud Giroud
Michel Gribi
Salomé Grisard
Sylvain Grimplet
Didier Grisoni
Anne Guglielmetti
Antoine Hahne
Olivier Hofmann
Dominique Huguet
Eduardo Hunziker
Juan Ignacio Ramos
Pierre Jacquier
Michel Kaeppeli
Matthis Kalbermatten
Matthias Kohler
Félix Krenz
Stéphane Kury
Elise Lammer
Patricia Leal Laredo
Patrick Longchamp
Olivier Lyon
Frédéric Magnin
Alcibiades Manias
Christel Martignoni
Salvatore Mercuri
Catherine Moreillon
Christian Motte
Céline Mottet
Sarah Nedir
Sasha Nielsen
Andreas Oberhensli
Emmanuel Oesch
André Oliveira
Jong Jin Park
Gareth Pierce
Daniel Piolino
Michel Radovanovic

Olivier Rambert
Zahra Raymond-Ghazi
Cédric Richard
Gilles Richter
José Rodriguez
Pablo Roel
Thomas Rotzler
Alfred Rusterholz
Nathalie Saegesser
Raphaël Sauthier
Eva Sanchez
Nathalie Schlederer
Danielle Schmid
Ninetta Serse
Nermine Skroeder
Sandra Soehne
Béatrice Spahr
Barry Stanton
Martin Strauch
Sébastien Sterchi
Rodolphe Tacchini
Laurent Théodore
Mathieu Thibault
Jérémy Trieu
Philippe Trim
Mauro Turin
Bénédict Vanwely
Philippe Vauthey
Philippe Veluzat
Sandrine Wenker

AWARDS

2005   Richter & Dahl Rocha
Brunel Award, Commendation for Swiss National Train Maintenance Center,
Geneva Station, Switzerland

2005   Richter & Dahl Rocha
Best European Spa, First Prize for La Prairie Clinic,
Clarens-Montreux, Switzerland

2001   Ignacio Dahl Rocha, Premio Vitruvio

2000   Richter & Dahl Rocha
Distinction Vaudoise d'Architecture, Award for Nestlé Headquarters,
Vevey, Switzerland

1994   Richter & Dahl Rocha
ASPAN, Award for "Place sans nom" and "Espacité,"
La Chaux-de-Fonds, Switzerland

1990   Jacques Richter, "Europan" Entry Prize, Switzerland

1989   Ignacio Dahl Rocha, Biennale of Buenos Aires, Argentina
(with Billoch & Ramos)

1988   Ignacio Dahl Rocha, Finalist for Palladio Award, Vicenza, Italy
(with Billoch & Ramos)

1983   Ignacio Dahl Rocha, Architectural Excellence Award,
Yale University, New Haven, Connecticut, US

EXHIBITIONS

2003   *Espace Abstract*, Lausanne, Switzerland

2001   *Subtilités*, Archivio Cattaneo, Cernobbio (Como), Italy

2000   *Journées du Patrimoine*, Renovation & Transformation of Nestlé Headquarters,
Vevey, Switzerland

2000   *Forum d'architecture*, Fifth DVA, Lausanne, Switzerland

1998   Catholic University, Santiago, Chile

1997   Universidad di Tella, Buenos Aires, Argentina

1995   Yale University, New Haven, Connecticut, US

1995   Technical University, Berlin, Germany

1994   Museum Pasquart – Musée d'Art, Bienne/Biel, Switzerland

1989   Bienal de Buenos Aires, Buenos Aires, Argentina

MONOGRAPHS & EXHIBITION CATALOGUES

A Modern Move, Transforming Nestlé Headquarters in Vevey, Richter and Dahl Rocha architects (Basel, Berlin & Boston: Birkhäuser, 2002)

Building on Our Foundations (Vevey: Nestlé, 2000)

Richter et Dahl Rocha, Contemporary World Architects (Gloucester, Mass.: Rockport Ed., 1999)

Richter et Dahl Rocha, architectes 1990–1996 (Lausanne: Éditions RDR, 1997)

Espacité (Lausanne: Éditions RDR, 1994)

ESSAYS & ARTICLES

Walker, Robert. "Die Kur im Weinberg," *Hochparterre* 5 (Mai 2006): 66.

Hönig, Roderick and Werner Huber. "Die Grössten im Land," *Hochparterre* 4 (April 2006): 14–22.

"Clinique la Prairie SA 1815 Clarens-Montreux," *AS-Architecture Suisse* 160, 7 (2006): 31–34.

"Quarante aquariums sur le M2," *Bâtir* 4 (April 2006): 8–9.

"Richter et Dahl Rocha : une alchimie latino-helvétique," *L'Hebdo / Special Edition* (2006): 107.

"Departamentos frente al lago," *Summa+* 79 (II-April 2006): 90–95

"La Verrière," *Bâtir* 3 (March 2006): 16–17.

"Viviendas junto al lago, Montreux / Housing by the Lake, Montreux (Switzerland)," *AV* 116 (November-December 2005): 48–51.

Scaramiglia, Viviane. "Vaisseau de lumière : Une symbolique conçue à l'échelle humaine," *Tendance Déco* 5 (November 2005): 52–56.

Meyer, Philippe F. "Leçon de rattrapage: Immeubles résidentiels 'La verrière' à Montreux," *Faces* 61 (Winter 2005–2006): 47–51.

Mercé, Cayetana. "Ignacio Dahl Rocha: Richter et Dahl Rocha," *Summa+ Reportajes, Arquitectos y obras* (2005): 100–107.

"Le radeau de la Méduse," in *Concours international d'architecture pour le nouveau Musée cantonal des Beaux-Arts de Lausanne* (Lausanne: MCBAL, 2005): 100–107.

"Ignacio Dahl Rocha," in *Arquitectos Made in Argentina*, ed. Luis J. Grossman and Daneil O. Casoy (Buenos Aires: Arquitectos Argentinos en el Mundo, 2004): 29, 76–79.

"Fachadas de oficinas / office facades: centro de technología de producto Nestlé; IMD International Intitute for Management and Development; Route de Berne 46," *Summa+* 70 (December 2004): 206–222.

"Administration building in Vevey," *Detail* 5 (May 2004): 494–498.

"Richter et Dahl Rocha Architects," *Kult* (May 2004): 117–129.

"Un bureau face à la pluriculturalité," *AS-Architecture Suisse* 152 (2004): I–IV.

Pietrasanta, Monica. "Richter & Dahl Rocha," *OFX Archittetura* 75 (November-December 2003): 44–45.

"Richter & Dahl Rocha, Rénovation du Siège de Nestlé, Vevey, Refuge forestier, Vallée de Joux," *AS-Architecture Suisse* 146 (September 2002): 1–8.

Mercé, Cayetana and Ignacio Dahl Rocha. "Máxima restricción," *Summa+* 53 (February-March 2002): 52–59.

Mercé, Cayetana. "Nestlé (1996–2000): Restauro e intervención en un edificio moderno," *Summa+* 53 (February-March 2002): 60–65.

Mercé, Cayetana. "Rompecabezas de madera," *Summa+* 52 (January 2002): 108–111.

"Redefining the Box," *Perspecta 32 Resurfacing Modernism* (2001): 58–65.

Giordano, Maurizio. "Nestlé's New Headquarters: Between History and Contemporaneity," *OFX Architettura* 59 (April 2001): 98–109.

"Richter et Dahl Rocha, Nestlé Headquarters Renovation, Vevey, Switzerland, 2000," *A+U* 362 (November 2000): 108–123.

"À la recherche de l'intemporalité," *Architecture et Urbanisme* (December 1999): 66–68.

Della Casa, Francesco. "L'art de faire réapparaître un bâtiment," *SIA-Ingénieurs et Architectes Suisses* 15–16 (August 1999): 258–261.

Della Casa, Francesco et Manfred Miehlbradt. "Entretien ferroviaire: questions à Jacques Richter et Ignacio Dahl Rocha," *SIA-Ingénieurs et Architectes Suisses* 17 (September 1999): 292–299.

"Réhabilitation de siège social (Nestlé, Vevey, Suisse)," *Le moniteur d'architecture* 91 (March 1998): 90–92 .

Devanthéry, Patrick. "Faire peau neuve," Faces 42–43 (1997–1998): 42–45.

Dionne, Caroline. "La première étape d'une rénovation," *Fassade-Facade* 3 (August 1997): 29–35.

"Extention du siège administratif de EOS à Lausanne," *Archithèse* 4 (1993): 16–17.

Verding, Karl-Josef. "Junge Architektur für Europa," *Schweizer Baumarkt* 9 (June 1989): 3.

"Casa unafamiliare a San Isidro, Argentina," *Domus* 697 (1988): 1–2.

"Casa unafamiliare a San Isidro," *Abacus* 20, 5 (1983): 80.

SWHome® Housing System / Twin Villas
Competition: SWHome® Housing System, 1988–95
Project dates: Twin Villas: 1995–96
Location: Chailly, Switzerland
Client: Mr. & Mrs. Felley, Mr. & Mrs. Wiesel
Team: Kenneth Ross, Bernard Emonet, Christian Gonin, Alain Jaquenod,
Manuela Toscan

Prototype for a Forest Refuge
Location: "La Racine," Grand Risoux Forest, Canton Vaud, Switzerland
Project dates: 1991–96, Destroyed by fire 2003
Client: Cantonal Forestry Service, Vaud
Area: 25 square meters
Design: Kenneth Ross

Swiss National Train Maintenance Center
Location: Geneva Station, Switzerland
Project dates: 1995–99
Client: Swiss National Railway (SBB-CFF-FFS)
Area: 11,000 square meters
Team: Stéphanie Bender, Michel Paganin, Bernard Emonet, Christian Gonin
Structural Engineering: Frey & Associés SA; Boubaker Ingénieurs Conseils SA;
De Cérenville Géotechnique SA

Nestlé Headquarters / Renovation & Transformation
Location: Avenue Nestlé 55, En Bergère, Vevey 1800, Switzerland
Project dates: 1996–2000
Client: Nestec SA
Area: Renovation A Building (Jean Tschumi) 31,000 square meters / Liaison
Space 1,800 square meters / Offices 21,000 square meters / Communication
Floor 2,200 square meters / Lobby 1,200 square meters / B Building
(Burckhardt & Partners) Communication Floor 2,200 square meters
Team: Kenneth Ross, Christian Leibbrandt, Cédric Simon, Philippe Beboux,
Diego Behrend, Stéphanie Bender, Bruno Emmer, Bernard Emonet, Christian
Gonin, Daniel Hernandez, Eduardo Hunziker, Pierre Jacquier, Patricia Leal
Laredo, Carine Lombardi, Olivier Lyon, Liliane Mege, Salvatore Mercuri,
Barbara Moyano Gacitúa, Emmanuel Oesch, Manuel Perez, Gilles Richter,
Mathieu Thibault, Philippe Trim
Structural Engineering: Tappy Bornand Michaud SA
Facade Consultants: BCS, R. J. Van Santen
Landscape Architect: Christophe Hüsler
Exterior Lighting Design: AIK Expéditions lumière, Yann Kersalé

Nestlé Headquarters / Interior Design & Furnishings
Location: Avenue Nestlé 55, En Bergère, Vevey 1800, Switzerland
Project dates: 1996–2000
Client: Nestec SA
Team: Kenneth Ross, Cédric Simon, Patricia Leal Laredo, office furniture
system in collaboration with DAI Design

Nestlé Headquarters / Visual Communication Program
Location: Avenue Nestlé 55, En Bergère, Vevey 1800, Switzerland
Project dates: 1996–2000
Client: Nestec SA
Team: Kenneth Ross, Cédric Simon
Glass Logo Adaptation: Philip Baldwin, Monica Guggisberg, & Paolo Ferro
Exhibition Installation System: Kenneth Ross, Cédric Simon

Richter & Dahl Rocha Office / Renovation & Expansion
Location: Avenue Dapples 54, Lausanne 1006, Switzerland
Project date: 1999
Client: Richter & Dahl Rocha - bureau d'architectes SA
Area: 1,350 square meters
Team: Patricia Leal Laredo, Philippe Schmittler
Structural Engineering: Daniel Hernandez

Custom Furniture Designs for Hughes Chevalier, Inc.
Project dates: 1998–2000
Client: Hughes Chevalier Incorporated, Paris
Team: RDR design SA, Cédric Simon, Claudia Dell'Ariccia

Villa La Falaise / Renovation & Extension for UEFA
Location: Route de Genève 46, Nyon 1260, Switzerland
Project dates: 1999–2000
Client: Union of European Football Associations (UEFA)
Area: 800 square meters
Team: Stéphanie Bender, Caroline Dionne, Christian Gonin, Alain Jaquenod,
Philippe Vauthey
Landscape Architect: Atelier Acanthe: Gilles Clement, Frank Neau, Jacques
Bernus, Paysagistes
Structural Engineering: Bureau d'ingénieurs Pierre Roulet SA

Valmont Boarding School
Location: Route d'Oron 47, Lausanne 1010, Switzerland
Project dates: 1996–2001
Client: Congrégation des Sœurs Sainte-Marcelline de Milan
Area: Extension 1,550 square meters
Team: Christian Leibbrandt, Manuela Toscan, Alain Jaquenod, Philippe
Vauthey, Sandrine Wenker
Structural Engineer: Daniel Hernandez

Residential Development "Les Uttins"
Location: Rolle, Switzerland
Project dates: Buildings D, E, F, & G, 1998–2008
Client: SI Les Uttins sur Léman
Area: Buildings D, E, F, & G, 20,400 square meters
Team: Christian Leibbrandt, Bruno Emmer, Bernard Emonet, Antoine Barc,
Christian Gonin, Pouska Haessig, Pierre Jacquier, Miroslav Jandescek, Alain
Jaquenod, Martin Mouzo, Barbara Moyano Gacitúa, Hector Nunez, Michel
Paganin, Fabrice Roulin, Nathalie Saegesser, Philippe Schmittler, Manuela
Toscan, Philippe Vauthey
Structural Engineering: Urner & Associés
Landscape Architect: Jean-Jacques Borgeaud

New Learning Center, IMD
Location: Chemin de Bellerive 23, Lausanne 1001, Switzerland
Project dates: 1999–2002
Client: International Institute for Management and Development (IMD)
Area: 6,140 square meters
Team: Vincent Costa, Philippe Vauthey, Carine Lombardi, Daniel Piolino
Structural Engineering: Tappy Bornand Michaud SA
Facade Consultants: BCS

Villa Sager

Location: Jeddah, Saudi Arabia
Project dates: 1999–2007
Client: Sheik A. O. Sager
Area: 1,700 square meters
Team: Kenneth Ross, Patricia Leal Laredo, Adrien Barakat, Christian Gonin, Baris Kansu
Interior Design: RDR design SA, Cédric Simon, Claudia Dell'Ariccia

Nestlé Headquarters Company Store / Facade Concept

Location: Avenue Nestlé 55, En Bergère, Vevey 1800, Switzerland
Project date: 2002
Client: Nestec SA
Team: RDR design SA, Cédric Simon, Marco Turin, Antoine Baillie, Konstantin Tzonis
Consultants: Metal System SA

Nestlé Product Technology Center

Location: Lange Str. 21, Singen 78224, Germany
Project dates: 2002–03
Client: Nestec SA
Area: 11,500 square meters
Team: Kenneth Ross, Cornelius Boy, Christian Gonin, Santiago Pages, Philippe Schmittler, Olivier Wavre
Landscape Architect: Thomas Gnädinger
Structural Engineering: Fischer + Leisering

"Flon-Ville" City Hall / Competition

Location: Flon, Lausanne
Competition date: 2004
Client: LO Holding SA
Team: Kenneth Ross, Adrien Barakat, Mauro Turin

Office Building at Route de Berne 46

Location: Route de Berne 46, Lausanne 1010, Switzerland
Project dates: 2001–05
Client: Pierre Millet
Area: 4,700 square meters
Team: Kenneth Ross, Baris Kansu, Christophe Gachnang, Frédéric Comby, Didier Grisoni, Jong Jin Park
Structural Engineering: RLJ Ingénieurs Conseil SA
Landscape Architect: Sylvie Visinand

La Prairie Clinic / Extension

Location: Chemin de la Prairie, Clarens–Montreux 1815, Switzerland
Project dates: 2001–05
Client: Clinique La Prairie SA
Area: 7,320 square meters
Team: Christian Leibbrandt, Manuel Perez, Bruno Emmer, Bernard Emonet, Frédéric Comby, Dominique Giroud, Christian Gonin, Olivier Hoffman, Emmanuel Oesch, Fabrice Roulin, Nathalie Saegesser
Interior Design: RDR design SA, Cédric Simon, Claudia Dell'Ariccia, Juliane Mayor, Marco Turin, Konstantin Tzonis
Installation Artist: Daniel Schlaepfer
Landscape Architect: Jean-Jacques Borgeaud
Structural Engineering: Daniel Willi SA

Residential Complex "La Verrière"

Location: Avenue des Alpes 126, 128 & 130, Montreux 1820, Switzerland
Project dates: 2001–05
Client: Peter & Bernadette Brabeck-Letmathe, Christian Banse (Designated Project Manager)
Area: Building A: 4,165 square meters / Building B: 4,774 square meters / Building C: 1,906 square meters
Team: Martin Ioelster, Bruno Emmer, Philippe Vauthey, Bernard Emonet, Christian Gonin, Pouska Haessig, Alain Jaquenod, Carine Lombardi, Michel Paganin, Olivier Wavre
Visual Artist: Catherine Bolle
Structural Engineering: J.-F. Petignat Ingénieurs Conseils SA

New Meeting Place, IMD

Location: Chemin de Bellerive 23, Lausanne 1001, Switzerland
Project dates: 2002–05
Client: International Institute for Management and Development (IMD), Lausanne
Area: 2,100 square meters
Team: Barbara Moyano Gacitúa, Alexis Wintsch, Bernard Emonet, Hüseyin Araz, Christophe Gachnang, Alain Jaquenod, Michel Kaeppeli, Carine Lombardi, Jong Jin Park
Spatial study, and Furnishings: RDR design, Cédric Simon
Structural Engineering: MP Ingénieurs Conseil SA

pleinAir® Glass Partition System for Clestra Hauserman SA

Project dates: 2004–05
Client: Clestra Hauserman SA, Strasbourg, France
Team: Kenneth Ross, Cédric Simon, Konstantin Tzonis

Residential Development Im Forster

Location: Zurich, Switzerland
Competition date: 2004
Project dates: 2006–08
Client: Urs von Stockar & Monica Diez
Area: "Garage" 1,500 square meters / "Mittelberg" 8,200 square meters / "Gärtnerei" 6,100 square meters
Team: Kenneth Ross, Maria Losana Vela, Adrien Barakat, Xavier Depeursinge, Pablo Roel

New Museum of Fine Arts / Competition

Location: Chemin de Bellerive, Lausanne, Switzerland
Competition dates: 2004–05
Client: Musée cantonal des Beaux-Arts, Lausanne
Team: Kenneth Ross, Emmanuel Oesch, Pablo Roel, Nermine Skroeder, Diego Comamala
Structural Engineering: Tappy Bornand Michaud SA

Credit Suisse Regional Headquarters / Renovation & Transformation

Location: Lion d'Or 5–7, Lausanne 1003, Switzerland
Project dates: 2001–06
Client: Credit Suisse
Area: 5,400 square meters
Team: Christian Leibbrandt, Manuela Toscan, Claude-Alain Bieri, Bernard Emonet, Cornelius Boy, Christophe Gachnang, Pouska Haessig, Olivier Hoffman, Alain Jaquenod, Mathias Kalbermatten, Frédéric Magnin, Hector Nunez, Michel Paganin, Manuel Perez, Nathalie Saegesser, Rafael Sauthier, Sebastien Sterchi
Exterior Lighting Design: Light Cibles SA
Structural Engineering: Daniel Willi SA

Nestlé Headquarters Restaurant & WellNes Center
Location: Avenue Nestlé 55, En Bergère, Vevey 1800, Switzerland
Competition date: 2004
Project dates: 2005–08
Client: Nestec SA
Area: 4,510 square meters
Team: Kenneth Ross, Olivier Wavre, Christophe Gachnang, Mark Chaille, Eva
Sanchez, Sébastien Sterchi, Diego Comamala
Interior Design: RDR design SA, Cédric Simon, Claudia Dell'Ariccia
Structural Engineering: Tappy Bornand Michaud SA

Flon Les Mercier / Facade Concept
Location: Voie du chariot 3, 4, 5 & 7, Lausanne 1003, Switzerland
Project dates: 2006–08
Client: LO Holding SA
Team: Kenneth Ross, Diego Comamala, Maria Losana Vela

PHOTO CREDITS

Yves André: pp. 45, 47, 48, 49, 50, 51, 52, 53, 55, 56, 57, 60, 61, 62, 63,
64, 67, 68, 69, 70, 71, 72, 73, 76, 77, 78, 79, 83, 85, 86, 87, 90, 91, 93,
95, 96, 97, 99, 100, 101, 102, 103, 106, 107, 109, 111, 112, 113, 117, 128,
141, 142, 144, 145, 147, 149, 151, 152, 153, 154, 155, 157, 158, 159, 160,
162, 163, 164, 165, 167, 168, 169, 171, 172, 173, 174, 175, 177, 178, 179,
180, 181, 182, 185, 186, 187, 189, 191, 192, 193, 205, 207, 209 (bottom),
210, 211

Mario Carrieri: pp. 74, 75

Jean-Michel Landecy: pp. 105, 110, 114, 115, 119, 121, 122, 123, 131, 132,
133, 134

Olivier Wavre: p. 212

Hughes Chevalier Inc. (Paris): pp. 88, 89

Clestra Hauserman SA (Strasbourg): pp. 194, 195, 196

We wish to express our profound gratitude to Jorge Francisco Liernur for his involvement and invaluable contribution to this book. His essay brings to the forefront questions concerning the practice of architecture which we believe are crucial.

Our thanks goes to the editor Andreas Müller for his faith in the project and for his patient and enlightened supervision, and to Werner Handschin at Birkhäuser and to the copy editor Michael Wachholz for their great diligence and cooperation.

We would also like to thank those who collaborated on the making of this book, especially Caroline Dionne, for her unwavering dedication to the presentation of our work in monographic form, and Marco Turin for his tremendous commitment to the graphic design. For her exceptional editorial work and care for the project, we wish to thank Denise Bratton.

Many people offered their input throughout the process, and among them, we would like to make special mention of Ines Zalduendo, who translated the introductory essay, and Janka Rahm and Teddy Cruz who both generously gave of their time to consult with Caroline Dionne and Denise Bratton all along the way.

For their collaboration on the production of graphic materials, we would like to acknowledge Barbara Moyano Gacitúa, Bruno Emmer, and Valentina Cambiaso, of Richter-Dahl Rocha y Asociados.

We sincerely thank our clients, without whose interest and confidence the body of work presented here would have been impossible to realize.

And finally, but by no means least of all, we wish to thank all of our collaborators at Richter & Dahl Rocha, RDR design, and Richter-Dahl Rocha y Asociados, for their day to day dedication to architecture.

Jacques Richter & Ignacio Dahl Rocha